MEET THE MASTERS

MEET THE MASTERS

THE MODERN CHESS CHAMPIONS
AND THEIR MOST CHARACTERISTIC GAMES

WITH ANNOTATIONS AND BIOGRAPHIES

BY
DR. MAX EUWE

TRANSLATED FROM THE DUTCH BY
L. PRINS

AND
B. H. WOOD

Essay Index Reprint Series

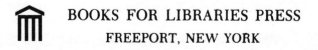

BOOKS FOR LIBRARIES PRESS
FREEPORT, NEW YORK

First Published 1940
Reprinted 1969

STANDARD BOOK NUMBER:
8369-1258-6

LIBRARY OF CONGRESS CATALOG CARD NUMBER:
78-90636

PRINTED IN THE UNITED STATES OF AMERICA

PREFACE

THIS is a translation of "Zoo Schaken Zij" ("They play chess like this") in which Dr. Euwe introduced the Dutch chess-playing public to the seven grand masters who were to participate with him in the famous A.V.R.O. tournament.

From the first we tried to keep close to his text, because it is so highly personal. Fate helped by losing our MS., which was addressed to us in Buenos Aires (where we were playing in the International Team Tournament) a few days before war broke out and has never been seen since. In correcting the proofs, we had consequently to refer back to the Dutch original throughout.

Herr Hans Kmoch rounded off "Zoo Schaken Zij" with a few paragraphs about Dr. Euwe himself, and this part of the book we have completely rewritten and greatly extended. It was almost impossible for Herr Kmoch to furnish anything his Dutch public did not already know; but we were in a very different position, and our British and American readers will be grateful for anything we can tell about Dr. Euwe. Our only further departure from the original is the addition of a few remarks about events subsequent to its publication.

Dr. Euwe has co-operated in the kind and warm-hearted manner typical of him. We also owe a debt of gratitude to Mr. J. Creevey for ungrudging help the correction of the proofs, to which labour Messrs. R. Blow, W. Ritson Morry, T. C. M. Olsen, and G. P. Smith have also contributed a noble part.

L. PRINS
B. H. WOOD

CONTENTS

CHAPTER VIII

CHAPTER IX

ILLUSTRATIONS

MEET THE MASTERS

CHAPTER I

WHAT DO THEY LIKE?

Before passing under review, one by one, the masters considered nowadays as leading challengers for the world's championship, let us make a general survey of the outstanding features of their individual styles of play. We intend to focus on the most noteworthy element in the style of each in turn and thus give a picture of the divergent methods which they adopt to attain their end.

By our question we really mean "What sort of position is the particular forte of each?" Here are the answers.

Alekhine: *Favourable Positions*

"Why," you might exclaim, "that is what every chess player desires. What is characteristic in this? You might as well say somebody has a weakness for wealth."

All the same, this is Alekhine's great characteristic. We shall show how he tries from the very outset to obtain, *and knows how to obtain*, a favourable position, and only when he has gained it gives his other powers full rein. Not without reason is he famed as a connoisseur of opening theory. To gain some advantage from the opening is vital to him, and he is willing to risk any difficulty or even hazard to attain, as quickly as possible, a position in which he feels at home. How often it happens that other masters miss opportunities through a faulty appraisal of the ratio of strength to weakness in their position! This ratio is rarely so exaggerated as one to nought; it may be five to four or eleven to ten, or even closer to equality. In this appraisal and judgment of almost incalculable situations Alekhine is unsurpassable. The ratio can be one hundred to ninety-nine and he will steer as confidently as ever for the more favourable of the positions offered him.

To profit from such minimal advantages, an extraordinary flair is required for conceiving and carrying through an attack. Alekhine has this indeed. His greatness is thus based on two foundations: genius in the creating, and virtuosity in the exploitation of, attacking chances.

He is the greatest attacking player of all time. Morphy has usually been given this title, but his task was much easier; in his time, about eighty years ago, people had naïve ideas about opening strategy. Morphy was the first great positional player; none of his opponents could approach him in this respect. Alekhine can; and the fact that his attacking skill still triumphs again and again amply justifies our description of him as unchallenged champion of the art of attack.

To understand Alekhine's greatness properly, one must—in view of the higher standard of play to-day— give the phrase "attacking skill" a wider interpretation than has been customary. How do we, and how used we to, recognize an attacking player, and on what basis do we assess his skill? Naturally on the way in which he decides his games; that is to say, on his technical ability. We admire his beautiful combinations, especially when they are prefaced by some sacrifice; the more frequent and striking the sacrifice, the greater our appreciation. This is an essentially old-fashioned criterion, for it confines itself to visible results, ignoring the mighty effort which must precede them. This latter is the most important, and nowadays is the decisive part. Ordinary mortals can envy Alekhine's genius in the discovery of charming and startling combinations; the more skilful player who feels himself quite capable of executing such combinations has a different feeling on the subject. To quote Spielmann, who is surely competent to pass an opinion on combinative skill: "I can comprehend Alekhine's combinations well enough; but where he gets his attacking chances from and how he infuses such life into the very opening—that is beyond me. Give me the positions he obtains, and I should seldom falter. Yet I continually get drawn games, even out of the King's gambit."

Well said, Master Spielmann! Alekhine's real genius is in the preparation and construction of a position, long before combinations or mating attacks come into consideration at all.

Capablanca: *Clear Positions*

The essence of Capablanca's greatness is his rare talent for avoiding all that can complicate or confuse the conflict. He is a realist who has banished the romantic and the experimental completely. In the attainment of positions which suit his style, or rather temperament, he exhibits almost mystical insight; as soon as the least cloud appears on the horizon, he alters his course so as to remain in clear water. He follows the sun, likes an easy life, is not sparing in offers to agree to a draw. To spectators this policy is not very attractive; he certainly draws an extremely high percentage of his games, the quickest often in unmistakably "grand master style," peace being signed before ever hostilities begin.

How, then, has he achieved such positive results? Wherein lies his power? Firstly, in the ability to perceive the remotest danger or the smallest opportunity far in advance; secondly, in the almost faultless technical perfection which enables him to hold on to an advantage once acquired with inexorable efficiency and convert it into a win. When he has to cope with opponents of equal stamp, he gets less frequent opportunities for this, since he does not set them too difficult tasks as a rule.

He can be regarded as the great master of simplification. The art of resolving the tension at the critical moment and in the most efficacious way so as to *clarify* the position as desired is Capablanca's own.

Flohr: *Quiet Positions*

Flohr's style recalls Capablanca's, but he lets the conflict become sharper. This reveals itself in his choice of opening, especially as Black. Like Capablanca, he tries to avoid complications; but, unlike him, he does not simplify at almost every opportunity. He is more patient and hard-working, and, whilst he likes *quiet* positions, does not go to extreme lengths to make them absolutely clear. Whereas Capablanca, if anything, is prone to simplify too soon, Flohr may simplify rather too late. His operations are slow as a rule. He is a specialist in jockeying for position, and in defence—eminent tactician as he is, he can permit himself this style. Only very rarely does he miss a favourable opportunity or fail to make the best of a difficult position. The opening is not his strongest point: he treats it quietly and solidly without setting such problems as Alekhine, but at the same time without Capablanca's covert fear of difficulties. He is no theorist, putting his faith in sound common sense. Psychologically, he is not so tense as Alekhine and not so fierce as Capablanca. He has repeatedly accepted an offer of a draw when in a decidedly better position, for instance, three times against Capablanca, at Hastings in 1934 and at Margate in 1936 and 1939, and against Reshevsky in the A.V.R.O. tournament—a thing which the world champions we have mentioned would never have done. You get the impression that, mere ability apart, he is quite content to demonstrate not his superiority over but his equality with the other leading masters. This explains why he draws practically all his games against the great masters, whereas he beats slightly inferior players with almost mechanical regularity.

Botvinnik: *Difficult Positions*

Every player has, sooner or later, to put up with a difficult position; Alekhine, for instance, very often. Botvinnik almost makes you feel that difficulty attracts him and stimulates him to the full unfolding of his powers. Most players feel uncomfortable in difficult positions, but Botvinnik seems to enjoy them.

Where dangers threaten from every side and the smallest slackening of attention might be fatal; in a position which requires a nerve of steel and intense concentration—Botvinnik is in his element. His style is anything but defensive; it is a mistake to assume that he accepts difficult positions so as to hold on to some small material advantage, as did Steinitz so often. On the contrary, his thoughts are always of attack. His method of preparing an attack is very characteristic; when he seems to be completely on the defensive he will be striving hard for a break-through, often through some deep combination. With devastating suddenness he is attacking—and like a master. Surprising switches like this are characteristic of his games, the whole situation changing in a flash. The preparations are made in secret; the explosion comes without warning. Flohr also often camouflages his real intentions so as suddenly to take the initiative, but the transition is never so dramatic as with Botvinnik. He often bases his plans on an advantage gained in the opening; he is an expert on opening theory, in which department he can be compared only with Alekhine, though his repertoire is smaller. It may be remarked that he is one of the few modern masters who cares to open with P–K4, a thing one can risk only if one knows the openings well, so varied are the ramifications which can begin with Black's first move.

Reshevsky: *"Boring" Positions*

Theory and practice, duly moulded by a player's temperament, combine to form the basis of his success. There may be little interplay between these factors.

Even leading masters have chinks in their armour; one may build up excellent openings but weaken in the middle-game, another may feel none too comfortable in the opening and consequently try to get away from well-trodden paths as early as possible; every player must allow for his own temperament, which will often force him to decisions quite indefensible on purely logical grounds. This is because practically every player has a penchant for a certain kind of position which he is only too happy to attain, and a distaste for some other type or types which he would like to avoid at all costs. This often leads to over-forcing of positions, with occasionally unexpected results.

Reshevsky is the exception—he is an all-round player with an all-round temperament. He has no partiality for any special type of position; he likes and plays every sort of game equally well; it is this which distinguishes him from his fellow-masters. Even positions which bore the others because there is—or seems to be—nothing at all in them he handles with as much keenness as another would devote to his special predilection. To Reshevsky, boring positions simply do not exist; in fact, our slogan for him might well have been corrected to "Positions which his opponents find boring."

He is above all a practical man, his play being simple and solid. His games give the impression that he does not seek for absolutely the best move, but is content if he finds a good one: that is, perhaps, unless the circumstances necessitate otherwise. He is an excellent tactician, seeing "stock" combinations at lightning speed, especially in defence, which brings out his combinative skill to the utmost. He does not originate sharp attacks or complications from choice. His inexhaustible patience enables him to hang on for hours and hours, his games often passing into lengthy endings. He has been called a specialist in the end-game, but this is hardly correct; his admittedly numerous successes there must be ascribed to tenacity and endurance rather than sheer talent. Naturally, the longer the game lasts, the greater the chance that his persistency and his equal partiality for any sort of position will bear fruit. Reshevsky knows this well, and consequently goes over into the end-game at every opportunity, even if he gets the worse of the position to begin with. Like his fellow-Americans, Capablanca and Fine, he has had plenty of experience of lightning chess. Of this he makes great use, often leaving himself fifteen or more moves to make within a few minutes, in a complicated and difficult position, whilst his opponent may have oceans of time; and yet he wins. The explanation is partly psychological. His opponent thinks—even though subconsciously—that it is impossible for Reshevsky not to make some blunder in such terrible time-trouble, and consequently he relaxes his own attention. Reshevsky was in time-trouble in twelve of his fourteen games in the A.V.R.O. tournament!

On the whole, Reshevsky's play is less deep than clever; less safe than diligent; less pretty than strong. His place among the foremost masters is fully deserved.

Fine: *Sharp Positions*

Fine is extremely gifted in the solving of technical problems such as the preservation of a small advantage;

but this is a characteristic of the younger players which he shares with Flohr and Reshevsky, not his own special perquisite. More typical is his readiness to go in for "chancey" positions, often enough in the very opening. He is not a combinative player like Alekhine, and his fondness for critical play is not so great as to make him take risks. No, he never takes risks! such is not in his style, though his straightforward, downright methods often force him to make moves which appear risky on the surface and give his play a keen edge. Unlike Capablanca, Flohr, and Reshevsky, he likes to confront his opponents with tricky problems from the very first move; not, like Alekhine, so as to get an attack, or, like Botvinnik, to produce the opportunity for a surprise counter-attack, but merely with an eye to position. Able technician that he is, he can exploit incidental chances as efficiently as he can carry through a routine attack. Above all, his play is logical. There was a striking instance of this in a tournament at Amsterdam, 1936, where he unexpectedly lost to one of the less fancied players in the first round. The tournament was a small one, so that he had little opportunity to make up his leeway. Another player might have played riskily, striving to wrest a little more out of his subsequent games—and very probably have overplayed his hand. Not so Fine; his play continued to exhibit just the same crystal-clear logic. He dropped a draw here and there, but by the last day he had reached top place.

Like Reshevsky, Fine is a highly experienced lightning player, and can achieve real marvels of efficacious play in the most severe time-trouble. One thing which does play him tricks now and then is his none too cool temperament, which bothers him more than the other masters; but if we are to make a considered decision, we must admit that his instinct for logic enables him to overcome this failing.

Keres: *Wild Positions*

Positions in which it is almost impossible to get one's bearings—there Keres is in his element. The wilder the better! This is a remarkable choice, for grand masters usually choose to avoid positions in which unexpected factors may enter to sway the conflict. They rely on skill rather than luck, and take a chance only when their game can no longer be held in the ordinary way. They leave the good, familiar path only as a last expedient. Keres, however, seems to prefer the desperate expedient to the safe path, quite apart from the question of necessity. So his methods contrast sharply with those of his fellow-masters. He is an attacking player of the first water, approaching Alekhine himself in this respect, with the great difference that Alekhine is consistently rational, whereas Keres is more irrational than not. He plays extremely well in wild positions, his penchant for combinations making him thoroughly comfortable in them.

Our remarks about "risks" must not be taken too literally, and we certainly should not like to give the impression that Keres is lost in anything but a scrappy game. He is a perfect grand master, equipped with every quality essential to a player of world repute. He knows the opening as thoroughly as the ending, and can treat any position on its merits. This distinguishes him from the wild attacking players of last century, but not from his contemporaries. The real hall-marks of his style are his preference for wild positions and the genius with which he handles them. It is an extremely attractive but also a risky style and carries with it the danger of unexpected setbacks. He will probably begin to play more sedately in the future, and when that happens his style will approach Alekhine's; if his development does take this trend, he may surpass all his contemporaries. At the moment, however, he merely plays differently, not more strongly. As he is the youngest of all the masters under review, his potentialities for the future must be regarded as the greatest.

Euwe: *Methodical Positions*

Napier once described Euwe as "an efficient maneating tiger." Alekhine contributed a far more searching analysis of his style in an article in the *Manchester Guardian* soon after the conclusion of the last world's championship match:

"Euwe's chess talent is in origin purely tactical—unlike that of such masters as Steinitz, Rubinstein, Capablanca, and Niemtsowitch. But he is a tactician who is determined at all costs to become a good strategist, and by dint of a great deal of hard work he has had some measure of success. The infallible criterion by which to distinguish the true from the would-be strategist is the degree of originality of his conceptions. It makes little difference whether this originality is carried to excess, as was the case with Steinitz and Niemtsowitch. In most of Euwe's games we find one and the same picture—a plan based on the formal data of the position, such as a majority of Pawns on the Queen's wing, an isolated Pawn on the opponent's side, combined action of the two Bishops, and so on. Generally the plan is good; but there are exceptions due to the tactical possibilities of particular positions, and these exceptions are by no means rare. Consequently Euwe as strategist stands at the opposite pole from where Reti stood. Reti declared in his famous book, *New Ideas in Chess*, that he was interested only in the exceptions; Euwe believes, perhaps a little too much, in the immutability of laws.

"What, then, in compensation for this slight shortcoming, are the assets which have made Euwe one of the most redoubtable players of our day? In the first place, his gift of combination. Does the general public, do even our friends the critics, realize that Euwe has virtually never made an unsound combination? He may, of course, occasionally fail to take account, or to take sufficient account, of an opponent's combination; but when he has the initiative in a tactical operation his calculation is to all intents impeccable.

"His other, and his principal, asset is undoubtedly his profound knowledge of the openings."

Much of this is very searching analysis indeed, as is of course to be expected from a man who, by his own confession, had studied Euwe's games and writings to exhaustion over a period of several months. It epitomizes the strengths and weaknesses in Euwe's play that the match revealed.

Why did Euwe lose that match? Simply and solely because Alekhine managed, frequently enough for his purpose, to bring about positions in which Euwe did not feel at home. What sort of positions are those? Unmethodical positions!

Euwe will go down to chess history as the apostle of method. He is a Doctor of Mathematics, a qualified actuary, licensed to teach book-keeping, an accomplished boxer, swimmer, and aviator. He has written more books than any three other living masters put together. How does he do it? By ordering his whole existence like a railway time-table, dividing it neatly into water-tight compartments, applying to his life the same sort of disinterested logical analysis that another teacher of mathematics might reserve for his theorems alone.

Many a chess player collects game scores in a desultory sort of way; many a master studies the openings more or less intensively; but Euwe's wonderful file-index leaves all these efforts in the shade—it is the eighth wonder of the modern chess world. It was understating the case to talk of Euwe's "profound knowledge" of the openings; Alekhine was consistently outplayed in the openings throughout the match he won. So Euwe's application of method starts long before his games begin. Method rules his training, which blends the physical with the mental. How many chess masters put in, prior to an important match, an allotted time daily to bicycling and shadow-boxing, followed by a cold douche and a brisk rub down?

Method extends to his treatment of the middle-game; he has catalogued combinational possibilities to the depths, as his writings show. He has every standard sort of combination at his finger-tips, and rarely misses a chance to carry out the manœuvre which fits the position. This is far from saying that his style is mechanical;

he is brilliant in discernment of the precise chances that the situation offers, and he shows the greatest originality in the application of combinative ideas, even if those ideas are seldom original in themselves. His is the Q.E.D., not of a pedant, but of an Einstein. The weakness of this system, and indeed of his whole approach to chess, is manifested on those extremely rare occasions when another genius, such as Alekhine, manages to confuse the issue beyond measure. As a result of his perhaps too versatile life, Euwe has been able to build up no reserve of habit, no ability to judge a position almost by second nature. For every game of chess, serious or "skittles," that he has played in the whole of his life, Flohr or Fine or Capablanca or Reshevsky must have played a dozen. So that he is immediately handicapped as soon as a position begins to escape the orbit of exact analysis. He cannot fall back on instinct, because he has supplanted instinct by reason. He probes into the position as methodically as ever; given unlimited time, he could work out the theorem; but alas, his clock is ticking against him and he blunders—he has committed more blunders in good positions than any other chess master who ever lived. Or else, methodical even in misfortune, he realizes that he has not time to analyse the position in his own way, and deliberately makes a superficial move. This weakness was evidenced again and again in the course of the match.

He also suffers, like Tarrasch, from being such a great teacher. He is too willing to pour forth his richness to a greedy world and share with others the knowledge of his own discoveries.

Still short of forty, and taking care of himself as few people do, he has already evidenced his recovery from the blow to his self-confidence of losing the world's championship. His method—and his methods —will explore many another universe yet.

CHAPTER II

ALEXANDER ALEXANDROVITCH ALEKHINE

As lively and eventful as his play has been Alekhine's career. Did he shape his life, or did his life shape him? A question for the philosopher. He was born in Moscow on November 1st, 1892. His mother taught him the elements of chess, with obvious success, for he was attracted to the game from the first. Scion of a wealthy house, he was able to devote himself to his hobby intensively. Journeys abroad with his family advanced his education, his self-confidence, and his discernment. At the age of eighteen he had already participated in a strong international tournament at Hamburg, scoring a very reasonable degree of success with five wins, four losses, and seven draws. A year later at Carlsbad he did just as well (eleven wins, nine losses, five draws). Two years later, in Stockholm, he won his first international tournament, and in 1913 he topped the strong Scheveningen international tournament, from which time onward Holland began to play a big role in his career. In 1914 he tied with Niemtsovitch for first place in the championship of Russia; then immediately followed the great-master tournament of St. Petersburg, which ended with Lasker in first place, Capablanca second, and Alekhine third. These successes, and particularly the attractive manner in which they were gained, aroused the acclaim of the whole chess world. His genius was

DR. ALEXANDER ALEKHINE
World Champion

revealing itself at Mannheim in the same year; but, before the tournament came to an end, war broke out. The concluding rounds were suspended, and Alekhine, who was already practically certain of first place (he was actually given the first prize) was interned in Germany, together with some other Russian players, among them Bogolyubov. Thus his career was interrupted for the time being.

Towards the end of the year he was allowed to return to Russia, where he served with the Red Cross. For seven years nobody heard any more about him, but in 1921 he suddenly turned up in Berlin, not as a nobleman but on holiday as a poor refugee. Poor? Not really, for his most precious treasure, his genius for chess, was with him still; and, despite his vicissitudes, a richer genius than ever.

With his return to the arena after the war, his progress towards the world's championship began. It is hardly possible to catalogue here all the successes of the brilliant period which ensued from 1921 to 1927. Wherever he played he was backed to gain first place, and he achieved the expected practically every time. Only the then world champion Capablanca and the ex-champion Lasker could hold him. In London (1922) he finished second to Capablanca; in New York (1924) third behind Lasker and Capablanca (exactly as in St. Petersburg, 1914); and once again in New York in 1927 he had to relinquish first place to Capablanca. It is difficult to understand even this relative measure of ill-success, for his play was certainly not inferior to that of his two great rivals. Possibly psychological causes prevented his giving of his best when Lasker or Capablanca were among his competitors. Playing over his games, one is forced to the conclusion that he never rose to quite his best form in these particular events.

Alekhine's match with Capablanca, held in Buenos Aires in 1927, put an end to all uncertainty. After an epoch-making struggle, conducted with the utmost stubbornness on both sides, Alekhine gained the victory by six wins to three, with 25 draws, and assumed the title of world champion. So came the second phase in Alekhine's career to a close . . . as first phase one must regard his early days up to the outbreak of the war.

The next phase was one of inactivity, and inactivity again. Alekhine took part in no big tournament, and the only occasion on which his powers were really tested was in the match against Bogolyubov at the end of 1929, which he won convincingly by eleven wins to five, with nine draws. A few months later, at the beginning of 1930, he registered the most imposing success of his life from the point of view of technique, scoring an overwhelming victory in the very strong tournament of San Remo. He drew *two games only*, winning every other game against opponents who included the best players at that time, and finishing far ahead of the rest of the field. His wins in this tournament exhibited, one and all, the art of chess at its most perfect yet. A year later at Bled he scored a hardly less imposing success—from the point of view of figures alone. But here the luck was with him, and his won games were by no means so convincing as at San Remo. An even more evident decline was revealed by his games in the Berne Tournament of 1932; nevertheless he won first prize there too. This obvious fading of his powers induced Bogolyubov to challenge him for the world's championship a second time. The match took place in 1934, but Alekhine again won brilliantly (eight to three, with fifteen draws). A few weeks later he obtained another "first" at Zurich, and this in a style which dissipated all further rumours of declining powers.

The period 1935–7, bounded by his two matches against Euwe, may be regarded as the fourth phase in his career, the period of his being an "ex-world champion." This phase is described elsewhere.

Nowadays Alekhine, the world master reborn, is in the fifth phase of his career, introduced by two beautiful tournament victories. A title match against Flohr was extinguished by the German annexation of Czechoslovakia, which country was financing the event.

Alekhine did none too well in the A.V.R.O. tournament; his partial lack of success might be ascribed to the excessive travelling involved. He has since turned down a challenge from the organizers on behalf of Keres on this same account, because they insist on play being conducted, in any tournament they arrange, in a number of widely separated centres in Holland.

His return match with Capablanca, awaited by the whole chess world ever since 1927, "nearly" arranged again and again, yet just as repeatedly called off, is definitely cleared off the board since December, 1939.

ALEKHINE AT HIS BEST

First Illustration

The criterion of a good move is its efficiency. There are hard-and-fast principles to teach us which moves are, and which are not, efficient in the openings; likewise, which *can* and which *cannot* be efficient. For instance, an early sortie of the Queen is usually condemned; only to be justified, in fact, when the opponent has made a gross mistake.

In the following game Alekhine brings his Queen into play early; seems to lose a lot of time moving her about and yet, although his opponent commits no definite error, gets a very good game. How is this? The explanation lies in his rare gift of judging every move, in every position, with perfect detachment. Even if there are a thousand general reasons for rejecting a move, Alekhine is always ready to consider it, and consequently often gets a chance to gain an advantage in a totally unexpected way. Here an obtrusive white centre Pawn exerts such pressure on Black's position that the white Queen can go safely into the very thick of the fight.

<table>
<tr><td>Dr. A. Alekhine</td><td>H. Wolf</td></tr>
<tr><td>White</td><td>Black</td></tr>
</table>

(Played in the tournament at Pistyan, 1922.)

IRREGULAR QUEEN'S PAWN

1.	P–Q4	P–Q4
2.	Kt–KB3	P–QB4
3.	P–B4	BP×P
4.	P×P	Kt–KB3

This symmetrical variation, though unpretentious enough on Black's part, makes it extremely difficult for White to extract any real advantage out of the opening.

5. Kt×P   P–QR3

An apparently harmless divergence from the symmetry which enables Alekhine to steer the game into quite a different channel.

6. P–K4!

Willingly accepting the opportunity—he hates symmetry for its drawing tendencies. This move is not without risk. White sacrifices his King's Pawn so as to retain his Queen's Pawn, which then, however, becomes isolated and could become weak. As compensation, the striking power of White's pieces is for the time being much superior to that of Black's, for various reasons: the King's Knight is well posted, the King's Bishop is free to come out, and the Queen's Pawn exerts pressure against the black position. For a player of Alekhine's style it is a congenial task to exploit this greater striking power of his pieces. This can be achieved only by combinative means, a circumstance which gives the game a most unusual flavour.

6. . . .   Kt×KP
7. Q–R4ch!

Forces Black to block the Queen's file so that the isolated Pawn is temporarily shielded from attack. Interposing the Queen (7. . . , Q–Q2) would be fatal, because of 8. B–QKt5.

7. . . .   B–Q2
8. Q–Kt3   Kt–B4

Black could alternatively have played any of the following moves: 8 . . . P–QKt4; 8 . . . Q–B2, or 8 . . . Kt–Q3. There is little point in examining the various consequences, for the same sort of game would have eventuated from each: violent attempts by White to hinder the normal development of his opponent's pieces. The text move has the recommendation that Black gains a "tempo" and at the same time guards his K3, a square vital for the sound development of his King's Bishop. However, there is a drawback too: the Knight on B4 is exposed to various threats.

9. **Q–K3!**

Tempting was 9. Q–KB3, to prevent Black's 9 . . . P–K3 through the concealed threat to his QKt Pawn. But this very move would have allowed Black to free his game by a little combination: 9. Q–KB3, P–K4!; 10. P×P (*e.p.*), Kt×P; 11. Kt×Kt, B×Kt; 12. Q×KtP, B–Q4, and White will have to sacrifice a piece to save his Queen.

By the move he chooses, White maintains the pressure

on K6 and in addition indirectly attacks the Knight on Black's QB4.

9. . . .   **P–KKt3?**

Compromising his game fatally. He should certainly have tried 9 . . . P–K3; for instance after 10. P×P, Kt×P; 11. Kt×Kt, B×Kt; 12. B–B4, and Black could defend himself by 12 . . . B–Kt5ch; 13. B–Q2, B×Bch; 14. Kt×B, O–O; 15. B×B, R–K1; whilst the keener continuation 10. P–QKt4, Kt–R5; 11. P×P, B×KtPch; 12. B–Q2, B×Bch; 13. Kt×B, B×P; 14. Kt×B, P×Kt; 15. Q×Pch, Q–K2, secures no clear advantage either. So White must reply to 9 . . . P–K3 with 10. Kt–QB3 or 10. B–B4, after which he would have only a slight pull.

10. **Kt–KB3!**

Alekhine employs his early developed Queen with incredible efficiency. This piece first of all cut off the attack on the Queen's Pawn (7. Q–R4ch); then threatened Black's QKtP (8. Q–Kt3), and finally checked the advance of the King's Pawn (9. Q–K3). With this move she attacks the unprotected black Knight and eventually renders it impossible for Black to castle on the King's side (11. Q–QB3).

10. . . .   **Q–B2**

After Black's preceding move, 10 . . . P–K3 is out of the question.

11. **Q–B3!**

Threatening not only 12. Q×R but also 12. P–QKt4 and consequently forcing Black to renounce all idea of castling on the King's side.

        11. . . .   **R–Kt1**

Necessary in order to reply to 12. P–QKt4 with 12 . . . B–Kt2.

        12. **B–K3**   **P–Kt3**
        13. **QKt–Q2!**

13. P–QKt4 would still get nowhere, because of 13 . . . B–Kt2! 14. Kt–Q4, Q–R2! 15. P×Kt, P×P; and Black regains his piece with a good position. 13. P–QKt4, B–Kt2! 14. B–Q4 would be met by 14 . . . B×B; 15. Kt×B, Q–K4ch.

        13. . . .   **B–Kt2**
        14. **B–Q4**   **B×B**
        15. **Q×B**

The skirmishes are over. There are no more acute threats in the position, and both players can turn their attention once again to developing their pieces. But

what a contrast there is between White's position and
Black's, for this purpose ! White can complete his
development in two moves (B–K2 and O–O) and there-
after, having a perfectly secure position, begin to
manœuvre on the open King's file or QB file, or both.
Black, on the other hand, cannot castle on the King's
side and cannot consider castling on the other. The
white centre Pawn impedes the most elementary
mobilization of Black's pieces. One can thus well
understand why Black fails to execute anything in his
next few moves but a hardly logical and perfectly
fruitless solo action by his Queen's Rook.

15. . . .   **B–Kt4**

To open up the Queen's Rook's file.

16. **B × Bch**   **P × B**
17. **O–O**   **R–R5**

White would have gone in for the forceful advance
of his Q KtP which follows, even had not his opponent
obliged with this attack on his Queen.

18. **P–QKt4**   **Q–Q1**
19. **P–QR3**

White has a positionally won game, and this in-
significant move does not alter the situation. "Insignifi-
cant" technically, such little moves have often a high
psychological value. They show the opponent how
powerless he is and undermine his morale. What
follows now is no fight; White commands a well-
organized army, whereas Black has merely a few
detachments scattered about at random.

Alekhine provides us with a little trimming: he finishes off the game combinatively by sacrificing the exchange.

19.	. . .	QKt–Q2
20.	KR–K1	K–B1
21.	P–Q6!	

A powerful break-through, with the ensuing sacrifice of the exchange already in mind.

| 21. | . . . | Kt–K3 |

On 21 . . . P–K3, White could win at least the Pawn on Black's QKt4: 22. Q–K3 (attacks the Knight) 22 . . . Kt–Kt2; 23. Q–Q3, R–QR1 (so as to counter 24. Q×QKtP with Kt×P); 24. Kt–K4, followed by 25. Q×P.

22. R × Kt!

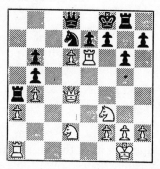

A lesser light might have discovered this sacrifice—but only Alekhine could have so brilliantly created the opportunity for it.

| 22. | . . . | P × R |
| 23. | Kt–Kt5 | Q–Kt1 |

There is nothing better: if 23 . . . P–K4; then 24. Q–Q5, Q–K1; 25. Kt–K6ch, K–B2; 26. Kt–B7ch, P–K3; 27. Q–B3ch, winning the Queen.

| 24. **Kt×KPch** | **K–B2** |
| 25. **Kt–Kt5ch** | **K–B1** |

Or 25 . . . K–K1; 26. R–K1.

| 26. **Q–Q5** | **R–Kt2** |
| 27. **Kt–K6ch** | |

So White regains the material sacrificed and remains a Pawn to the good with an even more crushing positional advantage than before. There followed—

27 . . . K–Kt1; 28. Kt×R dis ch, K×Kt; 29. P×P, Kt–B3; 30. Q×P, R–R2; 31. R–K1, Q–Q3; 32. P–K8(Kt)ch, Kt×Kt; 33. Q×Kt, Q×Kt; 34. Q–K5ch, K–B2; 35. P–KR4, R×P; 36. Q–K8ch, K–Kt2; 37. R–K7ch, K–R3; 38. Q–KB8ch, K–R4; 39. R–K5ch, K–Kt5; 40. R–Kt5ch.

Black resigns.

The value of this game lies not in the moves but in the ideas. The combinations are not particularly deep or unusual, but Alekhine's general strategy cuts right across all conventional lines. Who else would have realized that here existed the rare and exceptional case where very early mobilization of the Queen was strong?

Second Illustration

Curious is Alekhine's knack of developing a seemingly harmless attack, within a few moves, into a hurricane which smashes down all resistance. His methods are simple; it is not so much any particular move which is important, as the whole series of moves—and the move after that ! He is a poet who creates a work of art out of something which would hardly inspire another man to send home a picture postcard.

Dr. Alekhine   Dr. E. Lasker
White   *Black*

(Played at Zurich, 1934.)

ORTHODOX QUEEN'S GAMBIT

1.	P–Q4	P–Q4
2.	P–QB4	P–K3
3.	Kt–QB3	Kt–KB3
4.	Kt–B3	B–K2
5.	B–Kt5	QKt–Q2
6.	P–K3	O–O
7.	R–B1	P–B3
8.	B–Q3	P×P
9.	B×BP	Kt–Q4
10.	B×B	Q×B
11.	Kt–K4	Kt(Q4)–B3
12.	Kt–Kt3	P–K4
13.	O–O	P×P
14.	Kt–B5	Q–Q1
15.	Kt(B3)×P	Kt–K4
16.	B–Kt3	B×Kt
17.	Kt×B	Q–Kt3

Up to and including White's seventeenth move this game has been identical with several other games, including Euwe *v*. Flohr (Nottingham, 1936), after which it was demonstrated that Black can obtain a perfectly equal game by 17 . . . P–KKt3.

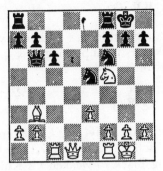

Now the real struggle starts. Alekhine has a little more freedom of movement, and his pieces, especially Bishop and Knight, are somewhat better placed than his opponent's. It requires the greatest skill to make anything of this slight advantage, but Alekhine succeeds. One would hardly expect Black to be checkmated within ten 'moves.

18. Q–Q6!

Attacking the Knight on Black's K4 and threatening, in some eventualities, Kt–R6ch, which would force a serious weakening of Black's King's wing if the Knight had to be captured.

18. . . .   **Kt(K4)–Q2**

18 . . . Kt–Kt3 would be answered by 19. Kt–R6ch P×Kt (now forced); 20. Q×Kt, but Lasker might have considered 18 . . . QR–K1, e.g. 19. Kt–R6ch,

K–R1, or 19. Kt–K7ch, K–R1; 20. Q×Kt(K5), Kt–Kt1! (not 20 . . . *Q–Q1*, because of 21. *Kt×P*).

   19. **KR–Q1**

Simple methods indeed; with every move—as is obvious—Alekhine is improving his position, every piece doing its bit.

   19. . . .   **QR–Q1**
   20. **Q–Kt3**

Threatening not only 21. Q×P mate but also 21. Kt–R6ch followed by 22. Kt×Pch and consequently forcing Black to weaken his King's wing.

   20. . . .   **P–Kt3**
   21. **Q–Kt5!**

Another strong move: among the threats is 22. R–Q6.

   21. . . .   **K–R1**
   22. **Kt–Q6**   **K–Kt2**
   23. **P–K4!**

White's invasion forms a beautifully co-ordinated whole. He plans to advance the King's Pawn to K6 and bring his Rooks into the direct attack on the King's wing, via the third rank.

   23. . . .   **Kt–KKt1**

Hoping to dislodge the white Queen from her dominating position by 24 . . . P–B3 or 24 . . . P–KR3.

   24. **R–Q3**

Frustrating Black's intentions, as soon becomes evident.

24. . . .   **P–B3**

24 . . . P–KR3 would be as useless: 25. Kt–B5ch, K–R2; 26. Kt × P, Kt × Kt; 27. R–R3, etc., or 26 . . . P–B3; 27. Kt–B5! P × Kt; 28. R–R3ch and mate.

Instead of the text move, Black would best have tried 24 . . . QKt–B3, with the following possibilities: 25. P–K5, Kt–K5; 26. Q–R4, Kt × Kt; 27. P × Kt, etc. Even then the passed QP should ensure an easy win.

25. **Kt–B5ch**   **K–R1**
26. **Q × KtP!!**

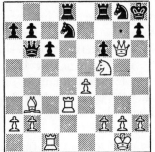

The miracle has been achieved. Black cannot avert mate. White's moves 18. Q–Q6! to 26. Q × KtP! form one magnificent unified conception. Only nine moves—and the race is run ! Everything unfolds harmoniously, everything goes equally simply; there is nothing diabolical, nothing smacking of sorcery. A good position always offers a choice of good continuations, and Alekhine might well have won in some other way; but had he diverged at any one move, then the combination could not possibly have formed such a splendid whole, or been so characteristically Alekhine's.

Let us now examine a few passages from Alekhine's games which aptly illustrate his combinative ability.

Firstly, two exactly calculated finales (Grünfeld–Alekhine and Alekhine–Rubinstein). In each there is already a win in the position, and it is "only" a question of driving this home. Any player knows very well how difficult a job this can prove in practice. To begin with, a plan has to be evolved quickly, for the critical phase of the game usually comes just when time is running short. There is no time for a detailed analysis of the position, taking everything into consideration. Intuition has to play a big part at such a time, which explains why great masters often let slip good opportunities. With Alekhine such a lapse is extremely rare; his talent for combination functions like a machine, and hardly ever lets him down. It is as if he heard a hidden voice: "Now is the time; now the combinations must start !" No sooner has he been warned than the combination is prepared.

It is still more difficult where the win is not yet forced, but the signs exist—it is "in the offing." Here, not moves must be found, but ideas, plans, inspirations—and here Alekhine rises to even greater heights. The Bogolyubov–Alekhine and Reti–Alekhine finales show how he handles situations like this. The wilder and more involved a position, the more beautiful the conceptions he can evolve. His game against Bogolyubov contains perhaps the most beautiful promotion combination in the whole of chess literature, whilst against Reti he first creates complications in rare style and then resolves them to his advantage.

Third Illustration

E. Grünfeld	Dr. A. Alekhine
White	*Black*

(Played in the Carlsbad tournament of 1923.)

Alekhine has just brought his Knight to the important square Q6, and his pieces are momentarily at their maximum of effectiveness. But White is ready to undermine the strongly posted Knight, so he must act immediately.

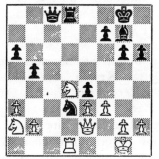

Alekhine sees his chance and wins by a neatly calculated combination—

30. . . .   **R × Kt !**

The simple 30 . . . B×Kt; 31. P×B, R×P; 32. P×P, Kt–B5; 33. Q–B3 would not effect anything worth while.

31. **P × P**

The alternative would have been 31. P×R, B×Pch; 32. K–B1 (32. *K–R1? Kt–B7ch*), 32 . . . Kt–B5! 33. Q–Q2 (33. *Q×KP, Q–B5ch;* 34. *K–K1, Kt×Pch;* 35. *K–Q2, B–K6ch*); 33 . . . Q–B5ch; 34. K–K1, P–K6!, etc. The text move seems to do all that is necessary, the Rook remaining *en prise* and the Knight being attacked now as well.

31. . . .	**Kt–B5!**

A surprise—

32. **P×Kt**	**Q–B5!!**

The whole point of the combination, and a magnificent idea very difficult to conceive beforehand. Black must win at least a piece.

33. **Q×Q**	

33. Kt—B3 would be hopeless, on account of 33 . . . Q×Q; 34. Kt×Q, R×R ch. If 33. R×R, not 33 . . . B×R ch; 34. K—B1, Q×Kt but—far more crushing—33 . . . Q×Q.

By 33. R–K1, Q×Kt, White would "only" have lost a piece; now it goes still worse with him.

33. . . .	**R×Rch**
34. **Q–KB1**	

Otherwise a whole Rook goes.

34. . . .	**B–Q5ch**

and mates next move.

This famous ending may be familiar to many of our readers but possesses an evergreen charm.

Fourth Illustration

Dr. A. Alekhine   A. Rubinstein
White   *Black*

(Played in the Carlsbad tournament, 1923.)

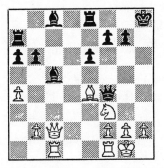

Alekhine's advantage in this position is different from that in the last. Black's position exhibits weaknesses on both wings: on the Queen's, the important square B6 is open to occupation, so that from it Black's QKtP, which can soon be rendered defenceless, can be menaced; and on the King's, the absence of the Rook's Pawn invites a mating attack. The latter is the more serious weakness, but to exploit it White must transport two pieces, one of them the Queen, across the board—not an easy task, because the black Queen is well posted to impede the process.

The plan Alekhine conceives is very simple in principle; he opens up the road to the King's side by means of a demonstration on the opposite wing, which draws away Black's active pieces (Queen and Rook). The fulfilment of this plan involves—typically of Alekhine—several surprising turns and neat finesses.

It is about ten moves deep, and of a remarkably forcing character—

21. **P–QKt4**   **B–B1**

Not 21 . . . B × KtP, because of 22. Q × B, R × Q; 23. R × Rch and mate.

22. **Q–B6**

Threatening Rook and Pawn. If Black replies at random, e.g. by 22 . . . B–Q2, there follows 23. Q × KtP, attacking the other Rook so that Black has no time to capture the Bishop. Therefore—

22. . . .   **R–Q2**

So as to save both the attacked units.

23. **P–Kt3**

This is really an attack on the QKtP, for, as soon as the black Queen ceases to threaten the Bishop, White's Queen is free to capture the Pawn. The text move has a rather remarkable second significance, as the sequel shows.

23. . . .   **Q–Kt1**

Black himself adds lustre to the game here by making the very best move and rejecting the simplifying 23 . . . Q–Q3. That also would lose, but the game would not then follow the main lines of White's plan. In *My Best Games of Chess* Alekhine gives two winning continuations against this alternative move, the simpler being: (23 . . . Q–Q3); 24. KR–Q1, Q × Rch; (34 . . . Q × Q? 25. B × Q, R × Rch; 26. R × R, R–K2; 27. R–Q8); 25. R × Q, R × Rch; 26. K–Kt2, B–Q2; 27. Q × KtP, B × P; 28. Q × RP, B–Q2;

29. Kt–Kt5, K–Kt1; 30. Q–K2, with a double threat
of 31. Q–R5 and 31. Q×R, which is unanswerable.

24. **Kt–Kt5**

Another sharp threat: 25. Kt×BPch (25 . . .
R×Kt; 26. Q×R).

24. . . .   **R(K1)–Q1**
25. **B–Kt6**

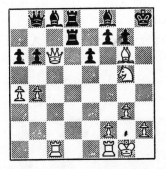

This astonishing move reveals White's plan in its
entirety. See how White, with his last three moves,
has cleared the way from QB6 to KKt2, from which
latter square the Queen clinches the win. Had not this
clearance been linked with a continuous series of
threats, Black would have had time to evolve a satisfactory defence. For instance, 25. B–Kt1 would have
been satisfactorily countered by 25 . . . Q–K4. The text
move is immediately decisive. Black is threatened with
loss of the exchange and a Pawn; if he captures the
desperado on his KKt3, he is elegantly mated: 25 . . .
P×B; 26. Q–Kt2, K–Kt1; 27. Q–R3, B×P (the only
move); 28. Q–R7ch, K–B1; 29. Q–R8ch, K–K2;

30. Q×Pch, K–K1; 31. Q–Kt8ch, B–B1 (31 . . .
K–K2; 32. *Q–B7ch);* 32. Q×Pch and mate.

       25. · · ·   **Q–K4**

Black submits to the loss of material. White now
wins simply and speedily: 26. **Kt×BPch, R×Kt;**
27. **B×R, Q–KB4;** 28. **KR–Q1, R×Rch;** 29. **R×R,
Q×B;** 30. **Q×B, K–R2;** 31. **Q×RP, Q–B6;** 32.
Q–Q3ch, Resigns.

Fifth Illustration

E. D. Bogolyubov   Dr. A. Alekhine
White   *Black*

(Played at Hastings in 1922.)
Position after 25. Kt(B2)–Q1.

Black is a useful pawn to the good, and his pieces
are, on the whole, more effectively posted; his Queen's
Knight commands the strong square Q6, and the
other can come to Q4 when the QBP is exchanged off.
White has not a lot of counter-chances: his best is the
possibility of advancing his Knight to K5 via QB4,

after which he might make something of the break-through by P–Kt4.

A stolid player might now concentrate on two things: preserving his passed Pawn and keeping the Knight on White's Q2 under keen observation. This plan would necessitate a series of laborious manœuvres not at all in the style of Alekhine, who solves the problem of the position in a vastly different way. His extra Pawn means little to him; perceiving how awkwardly, for the moment, White's pieces are placed for defence (the Rook at Kt2, the Bishop and both Knights), he asks himself only one question: "How can I break through into my opponent's position?"

He succeeds remarkably: it is neither his Queen nor a Rook which cracks up White's game, but the *Queen's Knight's Pawn*, which, aided by the sacrifice of all three heavy black pieces, advances to promote to a Queen in five moves or so and decide the game. The whole conception is a magnificent example of keen and exact calculation, in which the least inaccuracy would have led to disaster.

These remarks give a good clue to Black's first move—

28. . . .   **Kt–Q6**

Now White can win back his Pawn in any of three different ways—

(*a*) 29. P×P, B×P; 30. Q×BP;
(*b*) 29. P×P, B×P; 30. R×P;
(*c*) 29. R×P

The line (*c*), which was actually adopted, looks best because Black's Knight cannot make use of his Q4;

and yet (*a*) would actually have been better, **e.g.**
29. P×P, B×P; 30. Q×BP, Kt–Q4; 31. Q–Kt7,
B–B3; 32. Q–Kt1, and White might again make
something of manœuvring his Knight from Q2 to K5,
though Black would still have the better of it, quite
apart from the fact that he might have improved on
his earlier play, e.g. 30 . . . R–B2, instead of 30 . . .
Kt–Q4.

(*b*) is definitely inadequate: 29. P×P, B×P; 30.
R×P, Kt–Q4; 31. Q–R3, R×R; 32. Q×R, Q–B3,
followed sooner or later by . . . R–R1, with Black's
pieces filtering into White's weakly defended position.

> 29. **R×P**

The move on which Alekhine had based his plans.

29. . . .	**P–Kt5!**
30. **R×R**	**P×Q!**
31. **R×Q**	**P–B7!**

A brilliant climax: Black gives up, in turn, every
one of his three strongest pieces—the last with a
check !—to get his passed Pawn home.

32. **R×Rch**	**K–R2**

A difficult situation for White. Materially, even after the promotion of the black Pawn to Queen, he is not badly off; but his pieces are hopelessly misplaced for defence, and this is what Alekhine so clearly envisaged from the first.

33. **Kt–B2**

The only move.

33. · · ·   **P–B8(Q)ch**
34. **Kt–B1**   **Kt–K8**

Threatening mate on the move.

35. **R–R2**

Again forced.

35. · · ·   **Q × BP**

To follow up with 35 . . . B–Kt4. White cannot play 36. Kt–Q2, because of 36 . . . Q–QB8; 37. Kt–B1, B–Kt4.

36. **R–QKt8**

The only way to hold up Black's attack is to give up the exchange.

36. · · ·   **B–Kt4**
37. **R × B**   **Q × R**

Here the combination can be regarded as having reached its conclusion: Black remains with Queen for Rook and Bishop, with an overwhelming position into the bargain. The win can only be a matter of time. Alekhine played the ending no less elegantly and compelled his opponent's resignation after the following moves—

38. **P–Kt4, Kt–B6ch;** 39. **B×Kt, P×B;** 40. **P×P, Q–K7!;** 41. **P–Q5, K–Kt1;** 42. **P–R5, K–R2;** 43. **P–K4, Kt×KP;** 44. **Kt×Kt, Q×Kt;** 45. **P–Q6, P×P;** 46. **P–B6, P×P;** 47. **R–Q2, Q–K7!** (the promotion theme again); 48. **R×Q, P×R;** 49. **K–B2, P×Kt(Q)ch;** 50. **K×Q, K–Kt2;** 51. **K–B2, K–B2;** 52. **K–K3, K–K3;** 53. **K–K4, P–Q4ch.**

An extremely deep complication; yet in depth and complexity it is surpassed by the next, which has a psychological flavour in addition.

Sixth Illustration

One of Alekhine's outstanding characteristics is his determination. He may lose a game through over-playing his hand, but never through hesitancy or timidity. Yet his judgment of a situation is impartial, and he embarks on an attack only when he believes the position to justify it. There is only one exception to this rule: when he finds himself getting the worst of it, he immediately counter-attacks at all costs.

A beautiful instance of this, and also of the psychological aspect of his play, is provided by the following passage—

Position after 16 . . . B(Kt5)–R6:

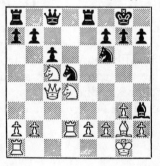

R. Reti   Dr. A. A. Alekhine
White   *Black*

(Played in the tournament at Baden-Baden in
1925.)

There followed—

17.	**B–B3**	**B–Kt5**
18.	**B–Kt2**	**B–R6**
19.	**B–B3**	**B–Kt5**

And Alekhine claimed a draw by repetition of moves.
Reti protested, and the tournament director ruled that
the automatic draw by repetition had not yet come
about.

The reporters wrote nothing about this; and some,
in reproducing the game, omitted the repetition completely, publishing scores reading 16 . . . B–R6; 17.
B–B3, B–Kt5; 18. B–R1. Yet the precise circumstances contribute useful evidence towards a correct
judgment of the situation.

Reti now went—

20. **B–R1**

and now Alekhine knew that, if he were to get a draw,
he would have to fight for it. He could see that White
had in mind an attack on the Queen's side, based on
the break-through P–QKt4–QKt5; the best chance,
in such a case, lies in counter-attack, as Alekhine is
the very man to realize.

There follows one of the most beautiful achievements of his whole career—

20.	**. . .**	**P–KR4!**
21.	**P–Kt4**	**P–R3**
22.	**R–QB1**	

White could not go straight on with his plan, as his
Queen's Rook was undefended: 22. P–QR4, P–R5;
23. P–Kt5? QRP×P; and wins.

22.	. . .	**P–R5!**
23.	**P–R4**	**P×P**
24.	**RP×P**	

By this exchange Black has weakened the position of
White's castled King: the fact that the KKtP is only
once protected soon gives Black combinative chances.

24.	. . .	**Q–B2**

Putting the weak point in White's position under
fire at once.

25.	**P–Kt5**	**RP×P**
26.	**P×P**	**R–K6!**

An offer which reveals the significance of his previous
move. 27 . . . R×KtP is threatened: 28. P×R,
Q×Pch; 29. B–Kt2, Kt–K6 and mate. 27. P×R
would be no defence. White is already thrown onto
the defensive.

27.	**Kt–B3**	

Not the best; preferable was 27. B–B3, which Alekhine intended to answer by 27 . . . R(R1)–R6, followed
by . . . R(K6)–QB6 in some eventualities. The text-
move reduces the Bishop to inactivity and also removes
the Knight to a less effective square.

27.	. . .	**P×P**
28.	**Q×P**	

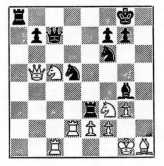

Now the real combination begins; we soon have an
almost fantastic number of pieces on each side *en prise*.

28. . . .	Kt–B6
29. Q×P	Q×Q
30. Kt×Q	Kt×Pch
31. K–R2	

31. K–B1, Kt×Pch; 32. P×Kt, B×Kt would
leave Black a Pawn up with much the better position.
What harm can befall White now? If Black captures
the Rook, White takes the Rook on K3, and there is
nothing in it.

| 31. . . . | Kt–K5!! |

A marvellous and far from obvious move. Three of
the four Rooks are now *en prise*; White must play
very carefully not to lose the exchange at once. For
example, 32. P×R, Kt(K5)×R and both 33 . . .
Kt×Ktch and 33 . . . Kt×R are in the air.

32. R–B4

Best, in the circumstances. 32 . . . B×Kt would
now allow 33. R×Kt(K4)!

32 . . . Kt×R; 33. Kt×Kt would be just as useless in view of the simultaneous threat against Rook and
Bishop.

. 32. . . .	**Kt×BP!**

Looks prosaic—Black wins a Pawn, and all the
threats suddenly disappear; but the most striking
passages are still to come. A single extra Pawn would
hardly carry the day in such a position, but Black has
worked out quite a distinct winning method.

33. **B–Kt2**	

Black threatened to win a second Pawn as well by
33 . . . B–K3 followed by . . . Kt×B.

33. . . .	**B–K3**
34. **R(B4)–B2**	

The best place for the Rook, as analysis confirms;
the attack on the Knights restricts Black's choice of
replies.

34. . . .	**Kt–Kt5ch**
35. **K–R3**	

Not 35. K–R1 because of 35 . . . R–R8ch.

35. . . .	**Kt–K4dis ch**
36. **K–R2**	**R×Kt**
37. **R×Kt**	

Forced; 37. B×R would cost him a piece.

37. . . .	**Kt–Kt5ch**

A little repetition of the same theme.

38.	**K–R3**	**Kt–K6 dis ch**
39.	**K–R2**	**Kt × R**
40.	**B × R**	**Kt–Q5 !**

It is all over. If 41. R–K3 or 41. R–KB2, then 41 . . . Kt × Bch; 42. R × Kt, B–Q4 winning a piece. White resigned.

A peerless example of Alekhine's attacking skill, remarkable for the many problem moves that followed the exchange of Queens. The position is incredibly complicated, and everything is suspended in mid-air; but Alekhine dominates the proceedings. He pulls the wires, and it is to his bidding that the marionettes dance.

Seventh Illustration

The last example showed a fine, complicated, and very deeply calculated combination which only began after the Queens had disappeared from the board. Such cases are rare, for a combination is, in its essence, a violent disturbance of the dynamical equilibrium, the chances of which are greatly reduced when the most powerful pieces are absent. One must not forget that the exchange of Queens started the complications off, so that these pieces played an important, even though preliminary, part.

Here follows an example of quite another stamp. Queens are exchanged off on the sixth move, when there can be no question of attack or combination. Nevertheless, it is not long before Alekhine's attacking skill shows itself, and though combinations are absent, the fight is tense enough for anybody's taste.

DR. A. ALEKHINE   R. FINE
White   *Black*

(Played in the Kemeri tournament, 1937.)

QUEEN'S GAMBIT ACCEPTED

1.	P–Q4	P–Q4
2.	P–QB4	P×P
3.	Kt–KB3	Kt–KB3
4.	Q–R4ch	

One of the newer forms of this opening.

4.	. . .	Q–Q2

This and the next move force exchange of Queens, leading to a drawn position, apparently—but it is not quite so simple.

5.	Q×P	Q–B3
6.	Kt–R3	Q×Q

This brings the Knight to a very strong position. 6. . . P–K3 was to be considered.

7.	Kt×Q	P–K3
8.	P–QR3!	

Played with insight. This move not only forestalls the check by the Bishop, which would force further simplification, but it threatens P–QKt4, which would cramp Black by preventing . . . P–QB4, his freeing move. If Black is to get in . . . P—QB4 at all, he must therefore play it at once; but this, as we shall see, puts him in trouble otherwise.

	8. . . .	P–B4
	9. B–B4	Kt–B3

Black cannot well avert the threatened 10. Kt–Q6ch, which will force off one of his Bishops.

	10. P×P

Before playing Kt–Q6, White takes the opportunity to gain several moves on his opponent.

	10. . . .	B×P
	11. P–QKt4	B–K2
	12. P–Kt5 !	

Alekhine extracts every ounce of advantage from the position.

	12. . . .	Kt–QKt1
	13. Kt–Q6ch	B×Kt
	14. B×B	

The opening is over, and Alekhine, once again, has achieved his primary aim—a favourable position.

Again it was not any particular move, but a coherent series of moves, each simple in itself, which brought this about.

The apparently innocent 8. P–QR3 forced, as we have seen, the *immediate* advance of the black QBP, creating a weakness at Black's Q3 which was shown up by 9. B–B4. Now White has the small advantage of two Bishops against Bishop and Knight, but we shall see that this is not easily retained.

14. . . .	Kt–K5
15. B–B7	Kt–Q2

15 . . . P–QR3, fighting for counter-play along the Queen's Rook's file, was the correct move. White could hardly reply 16. P–Kt6 to much advantage, because it would give Black's Knight a free entry to his QB3.

16. Kt–Q4

Extremely strong; White intends to place his Pawns on KB3 and K4, denying Black the use of his white squares Q4 and K5 for his pieces. He already has a little advantage on the black squares (White's K5 and Q4) through possessing the only remaining black-square Bishop.

16. . . .	Kt–Kt3
17. P–B3	Kt–Q4
18. B–R5	

If 18. B–K5, then 18 . . . P–B3.

18. . . .	Kt(K5)–B3

18 . . . Kt–Q3; 19. P–K4, Kt–K6; 20. B–Kt4!
would also leave White well on top.

      19. **Kt–B2**

The final preparation for P–K4, preventing the
reply . . . Kt–K6.

19. . . .	**B–Q2**
20. **P–K4**	**R–QB1**
21. **K–Q2**	**Kt–Kt3**
22. **Kt–K3**	

Otherwise comes 22 . . . Kt–B5ch. The movements
of this Knight have been most remarkable; first it
went to Q4 to prepare P–B3; then it went to B2 to
prepare P–K4; and now it goes to K3 to prevent
Black's winning back the minor exchange by 22 . . .
Kt–B5ch.

      22. . . .   **O–O**

22 . . . Kt–R5, followed by 22 . . . Kt–B4 would
have been a little better: compare with our note to
Black's fifteenth. Alekhine contrasts with other great
masters in the great rarity of such little lapses. After
the text move White never permits . . . Kt–R5 again.

      23. **P–QR4!**

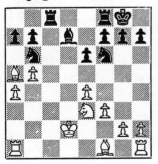

White, after 23 moves, has now only two pieces in play, and yet they are ideally positioned. The beautifully central post of the Knight on K3, the solid centre, the attacking formation on the Queen's side, the mobility of the Bishop on R5—these things make it impossible for Black to find good squares for his pieces, whereas White's pieces can develop their maximum combined effect within a few moves.

Situations like this are common in Alekhine's games. They draw one's attention to the distinction between "quantitative" and "qualitative" development. Alekhine always follows qualitative precepts, that is to say, he studies the effectiveness far more than the numerical strength of the forces at his command.

23.	. . .	KR–Q1
24.	B–Q3	P–K4

To free his Bishop.

25.	KR–QB1	B–K3
26.	R×R	

Not 26. B–Kt4 at once, because of 26 . . . R×R; 27. R×R, Kt×RP.

26.	. . .	R×R
27.	B–Kt4	

Preparing to push still further on the Queen's side.

27.	. . .	Kt–K1
28.	P–R5	Kt–Q2

Not 28 . . . Kt–B5ch, because of 29. Kt×Kt, B×Kt; 30. R–QB1, B–K3; 31. R×R, B×R; 32.

B–B5, P–QR3; 33. P×P, P×P; 34. K–B3 and Black
will soon lose his QRP.

29. Kt–Q5

29. R–QB1 might perhaps have been simpler, but
Alekhine avoids exchange of Rooks because end-games
with only the lighter pieces give many more drawing
chances. The text move gains White a passed Pawn
which, in connexion with his two Bishops, soon
becomes a powerful force. There is one slight flaw in
White's tactics: Black obtains control—even though
only temporarily—of his QB4, a factor which undoubtedly gives him some opportunities.

29. ...		B×Kt
30.	P×B	Kt–B4
31.	B–B5	R–Q1

A neat indirect protection of the Knight on his B4,
and certainly better than simplifying by 31 . . .
Kt–Kt6ch; 32. K–Q3, Kt×R; 33. B×R. The best
drawing chance lay in a fusion of these two ideas by
31 . . . Kt–Kt6ch; 32. K–Q3; and now 32 . . .
R–Q1 with the idea of continuing, after the attacked
Rook has moved, with 33. Kt–Q5. Even then, White
could maintain his advantage by 33. B–K7!

32. K–B3

Indirectly protecting the Queen's Pawn.

32. ...		P–QKt3
33.	P×P	P×P
34.	B×Kt!	

As is well known, the force of the Bishop-pair often lies in the possibility of exchanging back one of them for a Knight at the appropriate moment. By the text move, White obtains a second passed Pawn, which carries the day.

34. · · ·	P×B
35. P–Kt6	Kt–Q3
36. B–Q7!	

A beautiful finish. Black is completely helpless against the menace of B–B6, P–Kt7 . . . and R–R8.

36. · · ·	R×B
37. R–R8ch	Kt–K1
38. R×Kt mate	

The whole game is a beautiful example of Alekhine's great versatility in attack. Many other attacking players would have more or less lost interest when Queens disappeared so early, but not Alekhine ! He keeps up the fight right into the end-game, creating initiatives anew all the time.

Eighth Illustration

Now finally the game worthy of being considered the most important of Alekhine's whole career, and at the same time one of his best achievements in itself. It is the thirty-fourth and last game in his match for the world's championship with Capablanca at Buenos Aires in 1927. In winning this game he became world champion. To assess his victory in this match at its true value, one must recall that Capablanca was then considered absolutely unbeatable. Four times in succession, that is to say on every occasion when they had competed in together the same tournament (St. Petersburg, 1914; London, 1922; New York, 1924; and New York, 1927), the Cuban had finished above Alekhine, and there was not the slightest reason for considering Alekhine the stronger player. When this game began, Alekhine had a margin of two games (5–3) in his favour, but not everybody backed him to win even then. According to the conditions of the match, Capablanca required to win only two games to achieve an even score (5–5) and remain champion. It was at this critical stage of the match that Alekhine won game and title.

Not only for this was the game important; its technical execution was of the grandest. Alekhine obtains —as so often—a small advantage in the opening and then promptly confronts his opponent with a diabolical Queen move 21. Q–Q2! Capablanca misses the one and only obscure defence which would have held the balance of the position, and parts with a Pawn.

With the speedy disappearance of all but the heavy pieces from the board, it becomes most difficult for Alekhine to exploit his slight advantage: he has to be on the alert against all sorts of developments in which an odd Pawn would count for nothing. He solves his task with concentration, patience, and efficiency. Only in the very end, when he has an easily won game, does he relax a little and miss a chance of clinching victory a little more quickly—but this slight blemish we can well condone under the circumstances.

The most admirable feature of this game is the

superb technique by which a small advantage is converted into a win, a process which extends over nearly seventy moves against an opponent whose efforts, fraught with the energy of desperation, continually threaten to thwart him.

Having admired Alekhine for his combinative genius, let us conclude this chapter with this tribute to his inspired technique.

Dr. A. Alekhine   J. R. Capablanca
White   *Black*

(Final match game, Buenos Aires, 1927.)

QUEEN'S GAMBIT

1. P–Q4, P–Q4; 2. P–QB4, P–K3; 3. Kt–QB3, Kt–KB3; 4. B–Kt5, QKt–Q2; 5. P–K3, P–B3; 6. P–QR3, B–K2; 7. Kt–B3, O–O; 8. B–Q3, P×P; 9. B×BP, Kt–Q4; 10. B×B, Q×B; 11. Kt–K4, Kt(Q4)–B3; 12. Kt–Kt3, P–B4; 13. O–O, Kt–Kt3; 14. B–R2, P×P; 15. Kt×P, P–Kt3; 16. R–B1, B–Q2; 17. Q–K2, QR–B1; 18. P–K4, P–K4; 19. Kt–B3, K–Kt2; 20. P–R3, P–KR3.

21. Q–Q2!

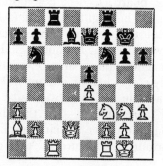

A typical Alekhine move which employs the Queen to her maximum of effectiveness. Black's position shows three weaknesses: on the Queen's side the unprotected QRP; in the centre the King's Pawn, and on the King's side the bad formation of Pawns at KKt3 and KR3. The text move strikes directly or indirectly at every one of these, as the following analyses demonstrate.

21 . . . R×R; 22. R×R, R–B1; 23. R×R, Kt×R; 24. Q–B3 and Black's King's Pawn falls.

21 . . . R×R; 22. R×R, R–B1; 23. R×R, B×R; 24. Q–R5 forking Black's Rook's Pawn and King's Pawn.

21 . . . B–B3; 22. Kt–R4! B×P; 23. Q–K3 winning a piece, since the black Bishop, in view of the possibility of Kt–B5ch, has to keep an eye on this square, so that 23 . . . B–B7 fails through 24. R×B.

21 . . . B–B3; 22. Kt–R4! Kt×P; 23. Kt(R4)–B5ch, P×Kt; 24. Kt×Pch, K–Kt3; 25. Q×Pch, K×Kt; 26. P–KKt4 mate.

This last variation in particular has a rare beauty and shows what subtle twists Alekhine can weave into a position.

21. . . .   **B–K3**

Subsequent analysis has revealed that only by the move 21 . . . Kt–R5! (recommended by Lasker) could Black have maintained equilibrium. Now he simply loses a Pawn.

22. **B×B, Q×B;** 23. **Q–R5, Kt–B5;** 24. **Q×RP, Kt×KtP;** 25. **R×R, R×R;** 26. **Q×P, Kt–B5;** 27. **Q–Kt4, R–QR1;** 28. **R–R1, Q–B3;** 29. **P–QR4!**

29. . . .   **Kt×P**

Tension again. White seems to get his Pawn back, but Alekhine has a surprise up his sleeve.

30. **Kt×P!**

Certainly not 30. Kt×Kt, Q×Kt; 31. R–QB1, because of 31 . . . R–QB1!, e.g. 32. Kt–Q2, Kt×Kt or 32. Kt×P, Kt–K6!!; 33. Q×Q, R×Rch; 34. K–R2, Kt–B8ch; 35. K–Kt1, Kt–Kt6dis ch and wins.

Alekhine is as adroit in avoiding his opponent's surprising attacking resources as in creating his own.

30. . . .   **Q–Q3!**

Best, in the circumstances. After 30 . . . Kt(B5) ×Kt; 31. Q×Kt, Q×Q; 32. Kt×Q the end-game would be easily won for White.

31. **Q×Kt**   **Q×Kt**

It is remarkable how everything fits in; Black could not play 31 . . . Kt×Kt, because of 32. Q×Pch, K–R1; 33. Kt×Pch winning the Queen.

32. **R–K1**   **Kt–Q3**

The only way to save the piece.

33. **Q–QB1**	**Q–B3**
34. **Kt–K4**	**Kt×Kt**
35. **R×Kt**	

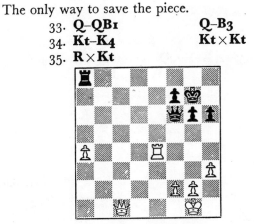

A very difficult end-game ensues, in which Alekhine converts his material advantage into a win in a most instructive way. When heavy pieces alone remain, it is very difficult to force a win. We shall present the remainder of the game in a series of snapshots, which best illustrate how Alekhine wends his way, through a series of end-game finesses, to victory.

35 . . . **R–QKt1**; 36. **R–K2, R–QR1**; 37. **R–R2, R–R4**; 38. **Q–B7, Q–R3**; 39. **Q–B3ch.**

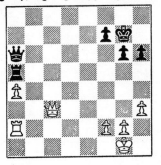

White has gained command of the long diagonal, and soon begins to operate with mating threats.

39 . . . **K–R2**; 40. **R–Q2, Q–Kt3**; 41. **R–Q7, Q–Kt8ch**; 42. **K–R2, Q–Kt1ch**; 43. **P–Kt3, R–KB4**; 44. **Q–Q4, Q–K1**; 45. **R–Q5, R–B6**.

And now White must not be over-hasty in his attack. For instance, 46. K–Kt2, R–R6; 47. R–Q8, which seems strong, would fail through 47 . . . R × RP!

46. **P–R4, Q–KR1**; 47. **Q–Kt6, Q–R8**; 48. **K–Kt2, R–B3**; 49. **Q–Q4**!

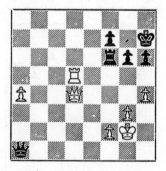

Forcing the Queens off in circumstances all to his advantage (Black's Rook cannot now take up its most effective position—*behind* the white Pawn).

49 . . . **Q×Q**; 50. **R×Q, K–Kt2**; 51. **P–QR5, R–R3.**

When the Queens leave the board, the passed Pawn becomes a personage of importance.

52. **R–Q5, R–KB3**; 53. **R–Q4, R–R3**; 54. **R–R4, K–B3**; 55. **K–B3, K–K4**; 56. **K–K3, P–R4**; 57. **K–Q3, K–Q4**; 58. **K–B3, K–B4.**

The Kings are fighting for space.

59. **R–R2, K–Kt4**; 60. **K–Kt3, K–B4.**

Sad ! the Pawn is too hot to touch; for if 60 . . . R×P, then 61. R×Rch, K×R; 62. K–B4, K–Kt3; 63. K–Q5, K–B2; 64. K–K5, K–Q2; 65. K–B6, K–K1; 66. P–B4, K–B1; 67. P–B5 and wins.

61. **K–B3, K–Kt4; 62. K–Q4.**

The white King swings off towards the other side; obviously Black is still worse off if he captures the Pawn now.

62 . . . **R–Q3ch; 63. K–K5, R–K3 ch; 64. K–B4, K–R3; 65. K–Kt5, R–K4ch; 66. K–R6, R–KB4.**

Now comes a rare event—Alekhine misses the strongest line. As he has stated himself, he could have

won by exhausting his opponent's good moves, **as**
follows: 67. K–Kt7, R–B6; 68. K–Kt8, R–B3;
69. K–B8! R–B6 (69 . . . *R–B4;* 70. *P–B4*); 70.
K–Kt7, R–B4; 71. P–B4 and Black can resign.

67. **P–B4, R–B4!** 68. **R–R3, R–B2;** 69. **K–Kt7,**
R–Q2; 70. **P–B5, P × P;** 71. **K–R6, P–B5;** 72. **P × P,**
R–Q4; 73. **K–Kt7, R–KB4;** 74. **R–R4, K–Kt4;**
75. **R–K4, K–R3;** 76. **K–R6.**

White sacrifices his Queen's Rook's Pawn to gain
Black's KRP.

76 . . . **R × RP;** 77. **R–K5, R–R8;** 78. **K × P,**
R–KKt8; 79. **R–KKt5, R–KR8;** 80. **R–KB5,**
K–Kt3; 81. **R × P, K–B3;** 82. **R–K7.**

Capablanca resigns and Alekhine becomes world
champion !

CHAPTER III

JOSE RAOUL CAPABLANCA Y GRAUPERA

J. R. Capablanca was born in Havana on 19th November, 1888. A curious analogy to Alekine's birth is presented by the fact that a match for the world's championship had been played there the year before. Steinitz played his return match against Lasker in Moscow; in Havana he had encountered Tchigorin. Again like Alekhine, Capablanca learnt chess at a very youthful age.

In 1900, when only twelve years old, he beat J. Corzo by four games to nil, with six draws, in a match for the chamionship of Cuba. This achievement is by no means to be minimized, for the standard of play in Cuba, as a result of the activity of the Havana Chess Club, was high.

Graduating from a secondary school, Capablanca went to New York to study engineering technique—and chess technique, although he had not originally intended it. He became a member and soon champion of the Manhattan Chess Club. In 1909 he defeated the American champion Marshall by eight wins to one, with fourteen draws, and thenceforth was accepted as the strongest player in the New World. This title has of course been challenged recently by Reshevsky and Fine, neither of whom, incidentally, he has met in a match.

Capablanca showed talent from the start, but more than this was needed to carry him into the foremost rank of chess greatness; he worked hard, especially in

JOSE RAOUL CAPABLANCA
World Champion 1921

the very beginning, to develop this talent. As with other great masters, his training blended study with practice. But there was a great contrast with Alekhine; Capablanca did not apply himself to opening theory (in which he never therefore achieved much), but delved deeply into the study of end-games and other simple positions which respond to technique rather than to imagination. It is said that he studied exhaustively more than a thousand Rook and Pawn end-games, a colossal undertaking for which he has been well repaid. His practical experience also followed a different course from that of the other masters of his generation. He participated in various tournaments in America, but the real measure of his theoretical knowledge was not the tournament game but the "skittle" game. Whilst a student in New York, he played thousands of rapid games, all for money stakes so that he was forced to concentrate; and this developed in him, in course of time, the superior positional judgment which later, in international tournaments, revealed itself as such a redoubtable weapon. Firstly, he learnt to play quickly without blundering; secondly, he developed the essential proficiency in wresting the clear positions he likes from every sort of situation. For years and years he never once got into time-trouble or into a position not under his rigid control. Only just recently has he deteriorated in this connexion; the time-devil does play him tricks sometimes, and altogether he makes harder going of it than of old.

Returning to the story of his career. His sparkling victory over Marshall speedily brought him inter-national renown. In 1911 he came to Europe for the

first time, to win first prize in the very strongly contested tournament of San Sebastian with six wins,
seven draws, and but a single loss. Immediately after
this he sounded Dr. Lasker, then world champion,
with the idea of their playing a match for the world's
championship, but matters never reached the stage
of definite negotiation. When Lasker won the St.
Petersburg tournament above him in 1914, beating
him in their individual encounter, his aspirations for
the title abated a little. Moreover, the war paralysed
chess for a while. Capablanca participated in three
tournaments only during the war (in New York, 1915,
1916, and 1918), winning first prize each time.
Returning to Europe after the Armistice, he redoubled
his efforts to obtain a title match with Lasker. After
several setbacks, among others the fact that Lasker
voluntarily relinquished his title, a state of affairs
Capablanca refused to accept, the match took place in
Havana in 1921, concluding with a victory for the
Cuban, who thus succeeded to the title. With the
score four to none in Capablanca's favour, ten games
having been drawn, Lasker adjudged the situation
hopeless and gave up the struggle.

    The new world champion well knew how to confirm
his standing by winning the great international tournament in London in 1922 with the shattering score of
eleven wins, no defeats, four draws. It was now that
he began to attract the description "unbeatable,"
yet within two years, at New York, his reputation suffered a sad blow: just as at St. Petersburg in 1914,
he had to be satisfied with second place behind Lasker.
Some consolation was afforded him by his surpassing

all the younger masters, and especially the "coming man," Alekhine. In the Moscow tournament he suffered another blow: Bogolyubov was first, Lasker second, Capablanca third; Alekhine did not compete. His only opportunity of crossing swords with the latter came in 1927 in the four-round tournament of six masters at New York; and here he scored an unchallenged first place, in front of Alekhine once again. Now his position as world champion seemed unassailable, the more so since Lasker had retired from active chess, and he could look forward to the title match with Alekhine, for which preparations were going forward, with supreme confidence. But, "vanity of vanities," the very first game brought the Cuban a cruel disillusionment. He was beaten—and as White !

This game was crucial for the match, as subsequently became evident, for Capablanca had been dislodged from his psychological throne and never once looked like recovering it throughout all the thirty-three games which followed. It is true he put up a mighty resistance, but he found himself on the defensive, and in chess—as in any conflict—success lies in attack. The "chess machine," by which admiring title he had been known, revealed the great drawback of a machine: it had not sufficient flexibility to adapt itself to altered circumstances.

Of the endless negotiations for a return match against Alekhine we have already written.

As ex-world champion Capablanca registered various successes; he came first at Berlin in 1928 and Budapest in 1929; second at Kissingen in 1928 behind

Bogolyubov; and, in company with Spielmann, behind Niemtsovitch at Carlsbad in 1929. He defeated
Euwe by two games to none with eight draws in a
match in 1931. After this he withdrew from the international arena for some time. His reappearance in
the Hastings congress of Christmas, 1934, was none too
successful, for he had to content himself with fourth
place. In Moscow a year later he finished fourth (to
Flohr and Botvinnik, equal first, with Lasker third).
Only in 1936, at Moscow, was he at last to know the
pleasure of surpassing Lasker in an international
tournament. He was easily first, and soon afterwards
in the strong Nottingham tournament he shared first
prize with Botvinnik. This really was a resounding
success. Then came the double-round tournament of
eight leading masters at Semmering-Baden, 1937,
where Keres won first place, followed by Fine,
Capablanca tying with Reshevsky for fourth place.

Even after his disappointing showing in the A.V.R.O.
tournament, in which he finished seventh out of the
eight participants, and his not very convincing second
place at Margate a few months later, we can still say
that he remains one of the best players in the world,
though he is obviously experiencing more and more
difficulty in maintaining his outstanding position. One
must not forget that he was the oldest competitor in the
Dutch tournament, and hence presumably the most
affected by the arduous travelling. He seemed too
inclined to seize material at the expense of position,
relying on his defensive skill to achieve the miraculous
—but his defensive skill can no longer always achieve
the miraculous.

CAPABLANCA HITS OUT

First Illustration

First of all, a game in the style that earned for
Capablanca the description "chess machine." We see
him obtain a small but definite advantage from the
opening, far from sufficient to produce a win of itself
but enough to enable him to cause his opponent
difficulties. The position is just to his taste: slightly to
his advantage, simple, straightforward. It is splendid
to observe how he holds his advantage and systematic-
ally increases it, exploiting each inaccuracy on the
part of his opponent. His unsurpassable efficiency produces a game which is a model of modern objectivity.

E. D. BOGOLYUBOV   J. R. CAPABLANCA
White   *Black*

(From the New York tournament, 1924.)

QUEEN'S PAWN GAME

1.	P–Q4	Kt–KB3
2.	Kt–KB3	P–Q4
3.	P–K3	P–K3

It is not in Capablanca's nature to seek intricacies
in the opening. This explains his choice of the quiet
3 . . . P–K3 instead of the keener 3 . . . P–B4 or
3 . . . B–B4.

4.	B–Q3	P–B4
5.	P–QKt3	Kt–B3
6.	O–O	B–Q3
7.	B–Kt2	O–O
8.	QKt–Q2	

8. P–QR3 is preferable: 8 . . . Q–K2; 9. Kt–K5.
This is soon apparent.

       8. . . .   **Q–K2!**

With the double threat 9 . . . P–K4 and 9 . . . P × P
followed by . . . B–R6. We see why 8. QKt–Q2 was
premature.

9.	**Kt–K5**	**P × P**
10.	**P × P**	**B–R6**
11.	**B × B**	**Q × B**

After the exchange of his Queen's Bishop, White's
attacking chances on the King's side disappear and he
has to be careful that Black does not take over the
initiative with the help of the open QB file. All this,
however, was common knowledge at the time. Bogolyubov presumably chose this variation to avoid
risks: a good policy in itself, for White has certainly
not got the worse game. But it soon becomes obvious
that Capablanca is far more at home in this clear sort
of position than his opponent.

12.	**Kt(Q2)–B3**	**B–Q2**
13.	**Kt × Kt**	**B × Kt**
14.	**Q–Q2**	

14. Q–B1 was the correct continuation, according
to Alekhine. White must make an effort to drive the
black Queen from her strong position.

     14. . . .   **QR–B1**
     15. **P–B3**

Weakens his Bishop's Pawn, which was well protected on the second rank. Better 15. Kt–K5 at once.

     15. . . .   **P–QR3!**

Beginning the real struggle. Black goes for the exchange of Bishops, which is to his advantage, as he has
the "bad" Bishop (moving on squares of the same
colour as his Pawns and therefore hampered by them)
and White the "good" one.

<pre>
16. Kt–K5   B–Kt4
17. P–B3
</pre>

Relatively best. 17. B×B, P×B would leave White
with two weak backward Pawns, his QRP and his
QBP. Nor would 17. P–QB4 be satisfactory, for
17 . . . P×P would leave him the choice only between
an isolated QP (if he recaptures on B4 with a piece)
or "hanging Pawns" (two Pawns united with each
other but isolated from their fellows—a dubious con-
figuration) if he recaptures with the Pawn. The text
move robs the black Knight of the use of his K5, to
which square it threatened to advance, attacking the
QBP.

<pre>
17. . . .   B×B
18. Kt×B   R–B2
</pre>

Black is now well placed, in view of the weaknesses in White's Pawn position, particularly the QBP, which can be attacked along the open file. White can easily protect the Pawn, but this implies other drawbacks and dangers inherent in positions in which one's opponent can continually threaten something or other. Experience teaches that in situations like this it is almost impossible for the defending party to find the best moves for ever if the attacker makes the most of his chances.

19.	**QR–B1**	**KR–B1**
20.	**R–QB2**	**Kt–K1 !**

The Knight is aiming for Q3, from which square it threatens to push on to QKt4 or KB4.

21.	**KR–B1**	**Kt–Q3**
22.	**Kt–K5**	

In the book of the tournament, Alekhine—whose excellent notes we are following here—shows that White could have put up a much more stubborn resistance by 22. Kt–B5, followed if necessary by Kt–R4.

22.	. . .	**Q–R4**
23.	**P–QR4**	

Here again White should have tried the manœuvre Kt–Q3–B5. The text move, presumably aimed against 23 . . . Kt–Kt4, produces a new weakening in White's Pawn position which is fatal.

23.	. . .	**Q–Kt3 !**

This simple move finally wins material as the outcome of a series of beautiful manœuvres, based mainly on the weaknesses in White's King's side. White's Queen's Knight's Pawn is attacked, and if he protects it then the weaknesses of his QBP and QP, one backward and the other pinned, are at once made apparent, e.g.—

(a) 24. P–QKt4, P–QR4! 25. P×P, Q×RP; winning either the QRP or the QBP;

(b) 24. P–QKt4, P–QR4! 25. P–Kt5, Kt–B5; 26. Kt×Kt, R×Kt; 27. R–R1, P–K4!; winning the QP;

(c) 24. R–Kt2, Kt–B4 (threatening 25 . . . Kt×P!); 25. R(Kt2)–Kt1, P–B3; 26. Kt–Kt4 (26. Kt–Q3, R×P! 27. R×R, Q×QPch, etc.); 26 . . . P–K4; again winning the QP.

Capablanca is no combinative player, but operations like this—"executive" combinations (in which an already existing positional advantage is exploited in the most mathematical way)—are his speciality.

24. **Kt–Q3**

Bogolyubov realizes he must lose a Pawn and gives up all idea of cutting across his opponent's plans. "Better late than never," he at last proceeds to transfer his Knight to QB5 but it is too late to save the game now.

24 . . . Q×KtP; 25. Kt–B5, Q–Kt3; 26. R–Kt2, Q–R2; 27. Q–K1, P–QKt3; 28. Kt–Q3, R–B5; 29. P–R5, P×P; 30. Kt–B5, Kt–Kt4; 31. R–K2.

Threatening 32. R×P; but the text move allows Black to crystallize out the position to a pretty win.

| 31. . . . | Kt×QP |
| 32. P×Kt | R(B1)×Kt |

White resigns, for 33. P×R, Q×Pch would lose the Queen (otherwise he is mated). Anything else would lose the QP.

Playing over this game, one gets the involuntary impression that chess is a deadly simple and easy game. This is true, after all—when you know how!

Second Illustration

The next game is of the same genre, but Queens are exchanged off in the opening, so that we have an unusually good opportunity of admiring Capablanca's skill in the end-game.

E. KAHN　　　　J. R. CAPABLANCA
White　　　　*Black*

(Played in the Moscow tournament, 1936.)

VIENNA GAME

| 1. P–K4 | P–K4 |
| 2. Kt–QB3 | B–B4 |

According to theory, 2 . . . Kt–KB3 is the best move here; but it leads to some most complex variations. Capablanca, never a connoisseur of the opening, prefers a modest line which produces the type of position he likes.

| 3. **Kt–B3** | **P–Q3** |
| 4. **Kt–QR4** | |

To win the "minor exchange" (Bishop for Knight). The sequel reveals, however, that this advantage is completely discounted by the opening of the QR file for Black.

4. . . .	**B–Kt3**
5. **Kt × B**	**RP × Kt**
6. **P–Q4**	**P × P**
7. **Q × P**	**Q–B3 !**

7 . . . Kt–KB3 would yield White a clear opening advantage through 8. B–KKt5.

| 8. **B–KKt5** | **Q × Q** |
| 9. **Kt × Q** | |

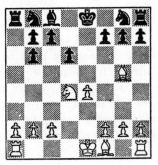

White has a respectable position, thanks to his two Bishops and his centre Pawn, which ensures for him a little more terrain. Black's task is now, above all, to prevent his opponent's posting his pieces aggressively, and Capablanca is just the man for this.

9. . . .		B–Q2
10.	B–B4	Kt–K2
11.	O–O	Kt–Kt3

This little move is important, preventing 12. P–B4, which would now be answered by 12 . . . P–R3; 13. P–B5, Kt–K4 winning a piece. Capablanca thus utilizes the incidental circumstance that his opponent's Bishop on Kt5 is more or less exposed, to post his King's Knight on a better square and prepare to castle, without wasting time with moves like . . . P–KB3 or . . . P–R3.

12.	P–QR3

The first effect of the open Rook's file. White has to waste a move with his QRP so as to free his QR and KB for action.

12. . . .		O–O
13.	QR–Q1	Kt–B3!

Once again, Capablanca seizes his chances in masterly fashion—chances, for the time being, merely of preventing White from taking the initiative. 14 . . . R–R5! threatens, after which White would have to say good-bye to his Bishop pair, e.g. 15. Kt×Kt, B×Kt (still more enterprising is 15 . . . P×Kt), and White must play 16. B–Q5, as 16. B–Q3 would succumb to 16 . . . B×P; 17. P–QKt3, B×B, and so on.

Another point of the text move is that 14. Kt–Kt5
would achieve nothing because of 14 . . . Kt(B3)–K4!;
15. B–K2, B×Kt; 16. B×B, R–R4; 17. B–K2,
Kt–B6ch; 18. B×Kt, R×B. This last variation illustrates prettily the significance of the factors we have
mentioned, the open Rook's file and the exposed position of the white QB.

14. **Kt×Kt**

Missing the best continuation. He should have
played 14. B–B1, posting this piece securely and pro-
viding extra protection for his QRP. 14 . . . R–R5
could then be answered by 15. P–QKt3, with P–QR4
to follow. The text move only strengthens Black's
Pawn position because it brings his QKtP to QB3,
where it commands his Q4, an important centre
square.

14. . . .	**P×Kt**
15. **B–Q2**	

Here again 15. B–B1 should have been given the
preference.

15. . . .	**R–R5!**

Eradicating one of White's two Bishops ultimately,
the reply being forced.

16. **B–Q3**	**Kt–K4**
17. **B–B3**	**P–B3**
18. **P–B3**	**R–K1**

Never lose patience ! Capablanca perceives well
that his opponent can no longer maintain his pair of

Bishops in any case, and therefore he is in no great hurry to exchange off his well-placed Knight.

19. **R–B2**

One might ask why White does not try to preserve his Bishop by 19. B–K2. The sequel supplies the answer.

19. . . .   **B–B1**
20. **B–B1**

A useless move which, however, does not give anything away.

20. . . .   **B–R3**

Now we see the point of Black's last few moves: White's KB is still exchanged off, but without leaving Bishops on opposite colours.

Black is obviously not playing for a draw.

21. **B×B**   **R×B**
22. **B×Kt**

Improving Black's Pawn position still further; but it is the best of a bad job. The Knight was strongly posted and a continual menace.

22. . . .   **BP×B**

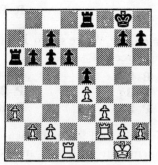

Now undoubtedly Black has the better of it. His
Pawns command more squares in the central zone, and
his Rooks can make more effective use of the open
files than White's. In addition, there is the possibility
of a break-through on the King's side by . . .
P–KKt4–Kt5, whilst White is condemned to pas-
sivity. Indeed, his only chance of a break-through is
by P–KB4, and this promises little, because his King's
Pawn, after the reply . . . KP × P, would become very
weak.

In the next part of the game Capablanca exploits
his chances very finely, but his opponent too knows the
ropes and makes a good fight of it.

23.	**R–Q 3**	**P–QKt4**
24.	**R(B2)–Q2**	**P–B4**
25.	**K–B2**	**R–R5**
26.	**K–K2**	**K–B2**
27.	**R–Q1**	**K–K3**
28.	**K–Q2**	**R–QKt1**

Both players have brought their Kings well into the
game. Black has posted his Queen's side Pawns
aggressively, preparing to break through on that side.

29. **R–B3**

Preventing 29 . . . P–Kt5; 30. P × P, P × P through
the concealed threat to the hinder black QBP.

29.	**. . .**	**P–Kt4**
30.	**P–R3**	**P–R4**

Black sees that he can achieve nothing decisive on
the Queen's side, so prepares for the break-through by

. . . P–KKt5, the most logical plan under the circumstances.

31. R–KR1

A good move. 32. P–R4! threatens, after which Black would have either to remain with a weak Pawn on the Rook's file (32 . . . P×P or 33. P×P) or to concede his opponent a strong passed Pawn on the same file (32. P–R4, P–KKt5; 33. P×P, P×P; 34. P–R5).

| 31. . . . | R–Q5ch |
| 32. K–K2 | R–Kt1 |

Preventing the advance 33. P–KR4, which would be countered by 33 . . . P–KKt5, to Black's benefit, since 34. P×P can now be answered by 34 . . . R×KtP.

| 33. R–Q3 | R–R5 |
| 34. R(R1)–Q1 | |

Black could try a break-through with P–B3 and P–Q4, were this Rook to remain on the KR file.

| 34. . . . | P–KKt5 |

The break-through succeeds, and the game now becomes critical, one of Black's Rooks filtering right through into White's position.

| 35. RP×P | P×P |
| 36. K–K3 | |

Not 36. R–KR1, because of 36 . . . P×Pch; 37. P×P (If 37. *K×P*, then 37 . . . *R–KB1ch*; 38. *K–K3,*

*R–KB*5, winning the King's Pawn) 37 . . . R–Kt7ch; and the Rooks become fatally effective.

36. . . .   **R–KR1!**

36 . . . P×P; 37. P×P, R–Kt7; 38. R(Q3)–Q2 would achieve nothing at all. Now White cannot capture the KtP because of 37 . . . R–Kt1, leaving White helpless against . . . R×KtP with . . . R×KP to follow. Black has made real progress with his last few moves, having gained the open Rook's file for his Rook. All the same, White is not yet lost.

37. **R–Kt3**   **R–R7**

White's KKtP is far more important than Black's QKtP. 37 . . . P–B3 would give White ample counter-play by 38. R(Kt3)–Q3.

38. **R–Q2**   **R–Q5!**

Now White may neither exchange Rooks himself nor allow Black to do so. The text move enables Black to protect his QKtP without having to reckon with an attack on his QP.

39. **R–K2**   **P–B3**
40. **R–B3**   **P–Kt6**

By sound manœuvring Capablanca has systematic-ally strengthened his position and now threatens to gain a decisive advantage by 41 . . . R–R8. But momen-tarily his KKtP is weak, a circumstance which (as Capablanca himself pointed out later) gives White a chance to save the game by 41. P–B4! This threatens

42. K–B3, winning the KKtP, and Black would therefore have to wind up the game summarily as follows:
41. P–B4! R–KR5; 42. P×P, R(Q5)×Pch; 43.
K–B3, R(R5)–B5ch; 44. K×P, R–Kt5ch; 45. K–B3,
R×R; 46. K×R(K2), R×Pch; 47. K–B3, R–R7;
48. K–Kt3! (so as to prevent 48 . . . *R–R6ch* followed
by . . . *R×R*); 48 . . . R anywhere; 49. P×P.
Drawn game.

Having missed this one chance, White is definitely
lost. . . .

41. **R–Q3?**   **R–R8!**

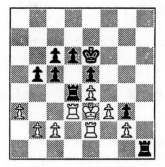

For the white King never gets another opportunity
to attack Black's KKtP.

42. **P–KB4**

Too late; this only hastens the end now.

42. . . .   **R–KB8!**

43. **P–B5ch**

Or 43. P×P, K×P, and the King's Pawn will soon
go.

43. . . .	K–B3
44. P–B3	R × Rch
45. K × R	P–Q4!

Gaining material. He threatens to exchange on his
K5 and capture on KB4 or, alternatively, to play
46 . . . P–B5ch and 47 . . . R–B5.

| 46. P–Kt3 | P–B5ch |

46 . . . R–QR8 was another winning line.

| 47. P × P | KtP × Pch |
| 48. K–K3 |

One last fling. White gambles on 48 . . . R–B8;
49. R–R2, followed by the advance of the passed
Rook's Pawn. Not 48. K–B2, P–Q5; or 48. K–Q2,
R–QR8.

| 48. . . . | R–QR8! |

Banishing all hope for White.

| 49. K–B3 | R × P |
| 50. K × P |

Or 50. R–K3, R–Kt6 and White is at a loss for
moves (51. K × P, P–Q5).

| 50. . . . | R × Pch |
| 51. K–R4 | R–B8! |

Black must not let the Pawn reach Kt5 supported.
52. P–Kt4, R–KR8ch; 53. K–Kt3, P–Q5; 54.
R–QR2, P–Q6; 55. K–Kt2, R–K8; 56. K–B2,
R × P; 57. K–B3 and resigns, for he must lose both
his remaining Pawns by 57 . . . R–B5ch; 58. K–Kt3,
K–Kt4.

An excellent game, highly characteristic of the
winner's play.

Third Illustration

The last two games revealed Capablanca as a positional player, firstly in the middle-game, secondly in the end-game. Here is a game in which he employed his positional advantage to build up slowly a decisive King's side attack.

J. R. CAPABLANCA   Dr. E. LASKER
White   *Black*

(The eleventh world's championship match game, Havana, 1921.)

QUEEN'S GAMBIT

1. P–Q4, P–Q4; 2. Kt–KB3, P–K3; 3. P–QB4, Kt–KB3; 4. B–Kt5, QKt–Q2; 5. P–K3, B–K2; 6. Kt–B3, O–O; 7. R–B1, R–K1; 8. Q–B2, P–B3; 9. B–Q3, P×P; 10. B×BP, Kt–Q4; 11. B×B, R×B.

Illustrating Lasker's preference for complicated positions. 11 . . . Q×B would have been better, to continue, after 12. O–O, with 12 . . . Kt×Kt; 13. Q×Kt, P–K4. Black chooses a line in which he experiences great difficulty in developing his Bishop..

12.	**O–O**	Kt–B1
13.	**KR–Q1**	B–Q2
14.	**P–K4**	Kt–QKt3
15.	**B–B1**	

Most players would have continued 15. B–Q3, 15. B–Kt3, or 15. B–K2 here. Capablanca has seen well that there is no better square for the Bishop than B1, where, incidentally, it waits patiently for 22 moves

before advancing into the battle. On any other square
it would have impeded the other white pieces.

15. . . .   **R–B1**
16. **P–QKt4**

Stopping . . . P–QB4. This move would not have
been playable had the Bishop retired to Kt3.

16. . . .   **B–K1**
17. **Q–Kt3**   **R(K2)–B2**
18. **P–QR4**

Before playing P–K5, White dislodges the Knight
from his Kt6 so as to prevent its moving straight to Q4.

18. . . .   **Kt–Kt3**
19. **P–R5**   **Kt–Q2**
20. **P–K5**

An advance whose consequences are very difficult
to assess. Capablanca demonstrates that giving up
control of his Q5 does little harm.

20. . . .   **P–Kt3**
21. **Kt–K4**   **R–Kt1**

As Capablanca remarks, this position is extremely interesting. Black threatens two things, mainly 22 . . . P×P. The best way of maintaining the pressure against Black's position would now have been 22. Q–R3. White's next move enables Black to post a Knight on his Q4; an operation, however, of little significance.

22.	**Q–B3**	**Kt–B5**
23.	**Kt–Q6**	**Kt–Q4**
24.	**Q–R3**	**P–B3**

Forcing White to exchange off Black's Bishop, which was threatening to come into good play via Kt3 or R4.

25.	**Kt × B**	**Q × Kt**
26.	**KP × P**	**KKtP × P**

Giving White more trouble than 26 . . . Kt(Q2) × P which would have allowed him easily to strengthen his position through his command of K5 and the weakness of Black's K3. Lasker makes the most of his difficult position, but does not succeed in equalizing.

    27. **P–Kt5**

Capablanca's remark here is typical: "White's exposed King's position invites an attack but, before embarking on this, White must exchange off his Queen's side Pawns to avoid possible subsequent weaknesses."

This is real Capablanca: he wants a clear position and would not think of starting to attack as long as his opponent has any sort of counter-chance. The question whether White's attack will be ultimately decisive or not is of less moment. The great thing is that he should be completely master of the situation.

27. ...	**R(Kt1)–B1**

Black can hardly interfere with his opponent's plan. If he plays 27 . . . P–QB4, then he is saddled, after 28. RP×P, RP×P; 29. B–B4, for instance, with a bad weakness on his QB3.

28. **KtP×P**	**R×P**
29. **R×R**	**R×R**
30. **P×P**	**P×P**

White has now attained his end; he has no longer anything to worry about on the Queen's side and can concentrate on the King's side attack. The passed black QKtP is harmless here, since Black cannot support its advance.

31. **R–K1**	

31. B–Kt5 would also have been good.

31. ...	**Q–QB1**
32. **Kt–Q2**	**Kt–B1**
33. **Kt–K4**	**Q–Q1**
34. **P–R4!**	

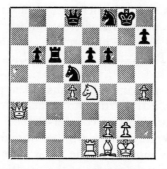

With his last four moves, White has built up a splendid attacking position. Nothing is directly threatened as yet, but one gets a feeling that a position so full of weaknesses as Black's here, with no prospect of rendering the King safer by exchange of Queens, must be untenable in the long run. According to Capablanca, Black should now have made an effort to save the game by 34 . . . P–R3, followed by . . . P–B4; but this does not seem to me to offer much hope. If 34 . . . P–B4 at once, 35. B–Kt5, R–B2; 36. Kt–Kt5, R–K2; 37. B–B4 puts White well on top.

34. . . .   R–B2

After this, Black is definitely lost, though the win for White is anything but easy.

35. Q–QKt3

Threatening 36. B–B4, which in turn threatens 37. B×Kt, P×B; 38. Q×Pch, Q×Q; 39. Kt×Pch; and 40. Kt×Q, winning two Pawns.

35. . . .	R–KKt2
36. P–Kt3	R–R2
37. B–B4	

With the same threat.

| 37. . . . | R–R4 |
| 38. Kt–B3 | |

Among the perils confronting Black now is 39. B×Kt, P×B; 40. R–Kt1 winning a Pawn. Black is consequently forced to exchange on his B6, a process which reveals the weaknesses of his position in a still clearer light.

| 38. . . . | Kt×Kt |
| 39. Q×Kt | |

Here begins the final phase in which White attacks the black King directly at last.

39. . . .	K–B2
40. Q–K3	Q–Q3
41. Q–K4	R–R5

4—(G.226)

41 . . . R–R2 could have been answered by 42. P–Q5:
P–K4; 43. B–B1, with B–R3 to follow. Now the
invasion of the white Queen decides the issue.

42.	**Q–Kt7ch**	**K–Kt3**
43.	**Q–B8**	**Q–Kt5**
44.	**R–QB1**	**Q–K2**

There is nothing better. 44 . . . Q–R6 would have
been refuted, as Capablanca shows, by 45. B–Q3ch
P–B4 (45 . . . *Q×B;* then 46. *Q–K8ch*, and 47. *Q×R,*
or 45 . . . *K–R3;* 46. *R–B7*, threatening 47. *Q×Ktch*
and mate); 46. Q–K8ch, K–R3; 47. R–K1, R–R1
48. R×Pch, Kt×R; 49. Q×Ktch, K–Kt2; 50
Q–K5ch with mate in a few moves.

45.	**B–Q3ch**	**K–R3**
46.	**R–B7**	**R–R8ch**
47.	**K–Kt2**	**Q–Q3**
48.	**Q×Ktch!**	

Black resigns, for he is mated in two moves.

This game too is most typical of Capablanca, fo:
it shows how, even when conducting a King's side
attack, he insists on getting a *clear* position.

Fourth Illustration

Up to now, we have seen only positional games by
Capablanca even though the last ended in a King's
side attack. So-called "attacking games," in which a
player goes, more or less riskily, for an attack from the
very opening moves, are not in Capablanca's line.
That he can also handle this sort of game excellently

too, if the occasion demands it, the following example
shows.

J. R. CAPABLANCA   V. V. RAGOZIN
White   *Black*

(Played in the Moscow tournament, 1935.)

NIEMTSOVITCH-INDIAN DEFENCE

1.	P–Q4	Kt–KB3
2.	P–QB4	P–K3
3.	Kt–QB3	B–Kt5
4.	P–QR3	

The Sämisch variation, a vigorous line whose merits
and demerits are difficult to assess and which Capablanca employs here because he happened to be
standing none too well in the list. White gains the
"minor exchange" at the expense of a doubled Pawn.
In order to deny Black the chance to exploit the doubled
Pawn, White must play energetically for attack, and
experience shows that he has fair chances. Not a
variation in Capablanca's normal style: he dislikes
having to assume obligations in the opening.

4.	. . .	B×Ktch
5.	P×B	P–Q3

5 . . . P–B4 is considered best.

6.	Q–B2	O–O
7.	P–K4	P–K4
8.	B–Q3	P–B4

But now 8 . . . Kt–B3 would be stronger. Black

must try to provoke the advance P–Q5 *withou.*
obstructing his QB4 square with one of his own Pawns.

9.	**Kt–K2**	**Kt–QB3**
10.	**P–Q5**	**Kt–K2**

10 . . . Kt–QR4 followed by . . . P–QKt3 and
. . . B–R3 would have been stronger.

11.	**P–B3**	**Kt–Q2**

11 . . . Kt–K1, threatening 12 . . . P–B4, would
have been much superior. White could not prevent
this last move by 12. P–Kt4, because of 12 . . . Kt–Kt3!
gaining full control for Black of his KB5, an important
square. So White would have had to continue with
12. Kt–Kt3, which seriously diminishes his prospects
of carrying out a pawn-storm on the King's side.

12.	**P–KR4!**

Since there is no threat of . . . P–KB4, White is in
no hurry over P–Kt4, but first seizes control of KR4.
12. P–Kt4 at once would have been unsatisfactory,
because of 12 . . . Kt–KKt3. Now, however, 12 . . .

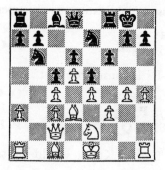

Kt–KKt3 can be comfortably countered by 13. P–R5
(13 . . . Kt–R5; 14. K–B2 threatening P–Kt3).

| 12. . . . | **Kt–QKt3** |
| 13. **P–Kt4** | **P–B3?** |

This should have been avoided at all costs, for it
lets White open a file for his Rooks on the King's
wing with ease. 13 . . . B–Q2 was indicated; for
instance 14. Kt–Kt3, Kt–R5, followed by P–QR3 and
P–QKt4. This would have offered some counter-
chances, although White's King's side attack would be
more dangerous than Black's counter-measures on the
opposite wing, anyway.

| 14. **Kt–Kt3** | **K–B2** |

The black King takes to flight, for his position at
Kt1 was untenable.

| 15. **P–Kt5!** |

Demonstrating the badness of 13 . . . P–B3?
15 . . . P×P would now be followed by 16. P×P, and
the black King could not return to Kt1 (desirable in
itself, since Black has now an open KB file for his
Rook) because of 17. Q–KR2 winning the KRP.

| 15. . . . | **Kt–Kt1** |
| 16. **P–B4** |

Permissible because of the insecure situation of the
black King. After 16 . . . KP×P; 17. B×P the
game would be opened up without Black's being given
any opportunity to make use of his good square K4.

| 16. . . . | **K–K1** |
| 17. **P–B5!** |

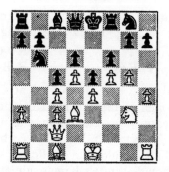

A position so curious that it deserves a diagram. It is a remarkable thing that White should have gained a decisive positional advantage after but seventeen moves of this keenly attacking game, although his King's side attack has come temporarily to a full stop.

17 ... **Q–K2**; 18. **Q–KKt2, K–Q1**; 19. **Kt–R5, K–B2**; 20. **P×P, P×P**; 21. **Kt–Kt7, B–Q2**; 22. **P–R5!**

To protect his Knight at its outpost and keep Black occupied with the threat of Kt–K6 for as long as possible. If Black were to advance his KRP, he would soon lose it.

22. ...	**QR–B1**
23. **P–R6**	**K–Kt1**

Black has virtually castled twice over; this time on the Queen's wing. His King is safe for the time being, but there is no chance whatever of any counterplay for him. He cannot attack White's weakened Queen's side by ... P–Kt4 without running risks through exposing his own King.

24. **R–KKt1, R–KB2 ; 25. R–Kt1, Q–B1 ; 26. B–K2, K–R1 ; 27. B–R5, R–K2; 28. Q–QR2, Q–Q1 ; 29. B–Q2, Kt–R5 ; 30. Q–Kt3, Kt–Kt3.**

After 30 . . . R–Kt1 (planning 31 . . . *P–Kt4*) 31. Kt–K6 would decide the game prettily. There is threatened not only 32. Kt×Q, but also 32. R×Kt!, Q×R; 33. Kt–B7 mate. 31 . . . B×Kt would be no defence, because of 32. QP×B, Kt–Kt3; 33. B–B7 and wins. 31 . . . Q–R4 fails in face of 32. R×Kt, and the only remaining move 31 . . . Q–Kt3 is smashed by 32. Q×Q! P×Q (forced); 33. Kt–B7ch, K–R2; 34. Kt–Kt5ch. Black must now leave his QP to its fate since 34 . . . B×Kt; 35. R×B leaves an un-answerable threat of gaining a piece by 36. B–Q1. The fact that, in two different variations, each of his Knights is stalemated and caught, reveals remarkably how helpless Black is.

31. **P–R4!**

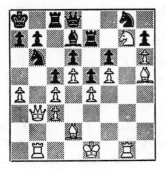

With this beautiful tactical finesse White returns to direct attack. He threatens to win a piece by 32. P–R5, and the Pawn is inviolate: 31 . . . B×RP? 32. Q–R2

(threatening 33. $R \times Kt$; if 32 . . . $Q\text{-}Q_2$, 33. $R \times Kt$, $P \times R$; 34. $B\text{-}Q_1$ and wins) 32 . . . B–Q2; 33. Kt–K6, B × Kt (forced); 34. QP × B and there is nothing to be done against 35. B–B7.

31. . . .	**R–Kt1**
32. **P–R5**	**Kt–B1**

Or 32 . . . Kt–R5; 33. Kt–K6, B × Kt (33 . . . $Q \times P$; 34. $R \times Kt$); 34. QP × B and the simultaneous threats of Q × Kt and B–B7 decide the issue.

33. **Q–R2, Q–B1;** 34. **B–K3, P–Kt3;** 35. **P–R6, Q–Q1;** 36. **K–Q2, Q–B1;** 37. **R–QKt2, Q–Q1.**

The Queen's shuffling repetitions are revealing. Black can do nothing but await the inevitable end.

38. **Q–Kt1**

Intending 39. Q–KB1 followed by 40. Kt–K6, B × Kt; 41. BP × B; and 42. B–B7.

38. . . .	**P–Kt4**

Fighting desperately for manœuvring room.

39. **P × P**	**Kt–Kt3**
40. **Q–R2**	**P–B5**

To prevent 41 . . . P–B4.

41. **Q–R3**	**Q–B2**
42. **K–B1**	**R–KB1**
43. **R(Kt2)–Kt2**	

Again threatening a decision by 44. Kt–K6. We now see how superb was Capablanca's judgment when

he left his Knight at KKt7 and went to protect it with
a Pawn, instead of playing it to K6 immediately.

43. . . .	**Q–Kt1**
44. **Q–Kt4**	**R–Q1**
45. **R–Kt3**	**R–KB1**
46. **Kt–K6**	

At last ! And now it is crushing. Black must
capture.

46. . . .	**B × Kt**
47. **QP × B**	**R–QB2**

So as to answer 48. B–B7 with 48 . . . R(B2)–B1.

48. **Q × QP**	**Kt–K2**

Or 48 . . . R–Q1; 49. Q × R(Q1), Q × Q; 50.
R × Kt, etc.

49. **R–Q1**	Resigns

Although the initial construction of this game was
hardly in Capablanca's usual style, it was not long
before he was sailing in familiar waters. The leisurely
way in which he pushed home his advantage, without
permitting his opponent a shadow of counterplay, is
typical of Capablanca. The positions remain crystal-
clear; from the brilliant combinations everything is
excluded that cannot be kept under strict control.

Fifth Illustration

We shall conclude with a game which reveals that
Capablanca can also produce brilliant combinations,
when they can be calculated out to the very end.
Many other masters combine less exactly. They trust

to general judgment of positions; sacrifice, for instance, without going any too deeply into the consequences. Capablanca does not trust—he calculates out. His extraordinary experience avails him well here: he works out a long combination in a flash, and can thus apply mathematical methods much more deeply than other masters. This is not to say that he does not occasionally make a move whose consequences are not exactly calculated; but this occurs rarely indeed.

J. R. CAPABLANCA　　　　N. N.
White　　　　　　　*Black*

STONEWALL DEFENCE

(Played in Havana, 1912.)

1. P–Q4, P–Q4; 2. P–K3, P–K3; 3. B–Q3,P–QB3; 4. Kt–KB3, B–Q3; 5. QKt–Q2, P–KB4; 6. P–B4, Q–B3; 7. P–QKt3, Kt–KR3.

The Stonewall opening is not particularly unfavourable for Black as long as he develops his Knights on Q2 and KB3, his KB on K2, and his Queen, perhaps, on K1. The way in which he handles it here is not so good.

6.	B–Kt2	O–O
9.	Q–B2	Kt–Q2
10.	P–KR3	

Threatening 11. P–KKt4 (11 . . . BP×P; 12. B×Pch, K–R1; 13. RP×P).

10. . . .　　　　　　　　P–KKt3

Now he can reply to 11. P–KKt4 by either 11 . . .
P×P or 11 . . . Kt–B2.

11. **O–O–O**

White, who already has the better of it, is aiming
for P–KKt4 at the earliest possible moment, e.g. after
12. QR–Kt1.

11. . . .   **P–K4?**

Black has a terrible game, but this practically loses
by force at once.

12. **QP×P**   **Kt×P**
13. **P×P**   **P×P**
14. **Kt–B4!!**

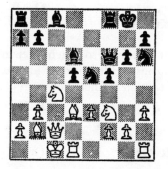

Introducing a deeply calculated combination, based
on all kinds of mating threats along the long diagonal.
A series of surprises follows.

14. . . .   **P×Kt**

Black has no good choice. If 14 . . . Kt×Bch;
15. Q×Kt, Q–K2; 16. Kt×B, Q×Kt; and then
17. Q–Q4 finishes the game. Black might have put
up a better resistance with 14 . . . Kt(R3)–B2, for
instance 15. Kt×B, Q×Kt; 16. Q–B3, Q–QB3 (17.
B–B4, P×B; 18. *Kt×Kt, Q–B3*); though he would
still be positionally lost in view of his weak Queen's
Pawn and White's two fine Bishops. Incidentally, not
through 17. Q×Q because of 17 . . . Kt×Bch; but
through 17. B–K2 or possibly 17. B–Kt5 !

15. **B×QBPch**   **Kt(R3)–B2**

Forced, for otherwise 16. R×B is still more deadly.

16. **R×B!**

The natural continuation.

16. . . .   **Q×R**
17. **Kt×Kt**

White has not sacrificed so much after all—only the
exchange, and it has yielded him an attack. The combination extends much farther, however.

17. . . .   **B–K3**

Forced.

18. **R–Q1**   **Q–K2**

The Queen must continue to guard the Bishop. If
she goes to Kt3, then White would win by 19. Kt–Q7
followed by Q–B3.

19. **R–Q7!!**

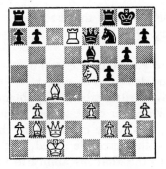

The point of the whole magnificent combination.
Black must take the Rook, as 19 . . . Q–K1 is refuted
by 20. Kt×Kt, threatening mate.

19. . . .   **B×R**
20. **Kt×B**

The main threat now is 21. Q–B3, which would win
at once after, say, 20 . . . Q×Kt. The other threat is
21. Kt–B6ch, mating or winning the Queen. (21 . . .
K–Kt2; 22. Kt–Kt4dis ch, K–Kt1; 23. Kt–R6 mate).

20. . . .   **KR–B1**

Black's only hope of continuing the game—but
it only serves to reveal the third link in White's
combination.

21. **Q–B3**   **R×B**
22. **P×R**

Black resigns, finding that 22 . . . Kt—Q1 would
lose the Queen by 23. Q–R8ch, K–B2; 24. Q–Kt7ch,
K–K3 (24 . . . K–K1; 25. Kt–B6ch); 25. Kt–B8ch,

K–Q3; 26. B–R3ch; and that 22 . . . Kt–Q3 would lose a piece by 23. Q–R8ch, K–B2; 24. Kt–K5ch; and 25. Q×R.

Such an achievement in the realm of combinative chess can only be described as superb.

After all I have written about Capablanca, perhaps you wonder how he ever came to lose his invincibility.

To my mind, this is the explanation: he perceives and calculates with incredible speed, but he became so accustomed to this that his ability to investigate a position with thoroughness diminished. "What he doesn't see at once, he doesn't see at all," a critic said once, and although this may have been said in jest, it has certainly a kernel of truth. Capablanca plays very superficially sometimes, in a way that can only be ascribed to lack of concentration. This is an integral weakness of his make-up and can only be partially compensated by his employing his time allowance to the full. But this leads to time-trouble and thence to other dangers, so that this inspired and speedy thinker is gradually involved in a vicious circle—superficiality, blunders in time-trouble, superficiality. . . . Now and then he succeeds in releasing himself from this vicious circle, and then he shows his old invincibility once again.

CHAPTER IV

SALO FLOHR

Salo Flohr was born on the 21st of November, 1908, at Horodenka in Russian Poland. About 1916 he came to Bohemia as an orphan refugee of the war, and this country adopted him as its own; a few years later he became a naturalized Czech. As a result of Germany's annexation of Czechoslovakia, he is now a refugee once again.

He grew up in the neighbourhood of Beneschau and settled down subsequently in neighbouring Prague. Various efforts to find a "civil" profession for him failed, but he gradually acquired a big reputation as a chess player in Prague circles. He learnt in a hard school, being condemned for many years to playing "skittle" games in small cafés for money stakes. To an even greater degree than in the case of Capablanca skittles formed the foundation of his play.

In 1928 he watched a big international tournament for the first time. It was at Kissingen, where a Czech chess journalist had brought him as an assistant. Few of the competitors in this tournament will recollect Flohr's presence, for the quiet little man kept very much to the background. However, it often happened that when the masters were analysing some game, this same quiet little man would come up and suggest a move which would make the great ones think. A few weeks later a big tournament was held at Berlin; again Flohr was present as an assistant journalist, but this time he was no longer unknown. In the Café

König, where the tournament was held, there was another room in which chess players regularly assembled. Every day, after lunch, a busy chess life developed, which only petered out, after strenuous struggles with the waiters, at about 3 a.m. Mainly skittles were played, for money stakes. Here was something just to Flohr's taste! He came, he saw, he conquered; and within a few days everybody in the place, not excepting three or four of the competing masters, was in his debt. He was well known to all the masters by now, but another year elapsed before the international public got to know of him.

After gloriously vindicating his private reputation in the Carlsbad tournament of 1929, he was invited to take part in the international tournament at Rogaska-Slatina held towards the end of the year. Here he won second prize behind Rubinstein and quickly gained the international limelight.

He did not score a really crashing success in the international field for some time. For instance, he could only finish equal third with Rellstab and Rejfir in the reserve tournament at Hastings in 1929–30. In the international team tournament at Hamburg in 1930 he scored a very promising result, being fourth with $14\frac{1}{2}$ points out of 17 (85 per cent) on the list of best individual achievements. In the Christmas congress at Hastings which followed, he topped the Premier Reserves with eight points out of nine. A year later (1931–2), he won the Premier section with the same score. Notable also was his good result in the team tournament at Prague in 1931. In the biggest tournament of the year (Bled, 1931) he did little, however,

SALO FLOHR
One of the ablest of the younger grand masters

tying for fourth place with Kashdan, Stoltz, and
Vidmar whilst against the three leading prizewinners,
Alekhine, Bogolyubov, and Niemtsovitch, he could
only score half a point out of six games.

As he gained more and more experience in the
routine of international master play his results improved and became more consistent, and since 1932
he has registered one success after another. For instance,
second prize at London (Alekhine first); equal first
with Vidmar in the strong tournament at Sliac, and
equal second with Euwe in Bern, behind Alekhine
again. A match against Euwe finished in a tie, each
player winning three games with ten drawn. In the
master tournament at Hastings (1932–3) he "naturally"
won first prize again, and he played brilliantly for his
country in the team tournament of Folkestone (1933).
He participated in a number of smaller tournaments;
for instance, at Scheveningen, where he won first prize;
in Hastings (1933–4) we see him once again at the top
of the list, with seven points out of nine; at Zurich
(1934) he came, just as at Berne, equal second with
Euwe behind Alekhine. In the latter part of 1933 he
had been playing an interesting match at Moscow and
Leningrad against Botvinnik, which ended in a draw
at two wins each, with eight draws. Then again in
the Hastings Christmas tournament of 1934–5 he tied
for first place with Sir George Thomas and Euwe, in
front of Capablanca, Botvinnik, and Lilienthal.
Striking was his success at Moscow in 1935, where he
tied for first prize with Botvinnik in front of Capablanca, Lasker, and a batch of other stars. It gradually
became impossible to broach the subject "world

championship" without Flohr coming to mind. Curiously
enough, as his reputation went forward, his playing
standard seemed to go back. At Christmas in Hastings
(1935–6) he had to satisfy himself with second place
behind the American Fine. It is true that he won the
Easter tournament at Margate in 1936 in front of
Capablanca, but the ensuing tournament of the élite
at Moscow was a big disillusionment. He was only
third, a long way behind the first two prizewinners
(Capablanca 13, Botvinnik 12, Flohr 9½). From this
blow he re-established himself at Podebrady, where he
finished first above Alekhine; but in a top-rank tournament at Nottingham in 1936 he experienced another
severe check. His 8½ points out of a possible 14 only
earned him seventh place, equal with Lasker. It is
only fair to add that he had a lot of bad luck in this
tournament, giving away two and a half points to
weaker opponents when he had built up overwhelming
if not winning advantages. It is very curious that he
should have lost, in the course of 1936, more tournament games than in the three previous years put
together. One hardly knows how to explain this. All
that is certain is that his opponents were not playing
unusually well, but that he himself did not seem quite
able, on these important occasions, to rise to his best.

His reputation as a candidate for the world's championship grew, and indeed it was soon given an official
standing. The summer of 1937 found Flohr playing
in the big Kemeri tournament, where he finished in a
triple tie for first place with Reshevsky and Petrov,
leaving other grand masters such as Alekhine, Fine, and
Keres behind. A few weeks later came the International

Team Tournament at Stockholm, and at the meeting of the International Chess Federation held there he was elected official candidate for the world's championship. Soon after, however, there came yet another disappointing result: in the tournament at Semmering-Baden advertised by the organizers as a "tournament for world championship candidates," he failed to vindicate his front-rank position. Out of the eight participants, he was fifth only (Keres 9, Fine 8, Capablanca and Reshevsky 7½ each, Flohr 7, Eliskases and Ragosin each 6, Petrov 5). Nor did he succeed in adding another to his series of first prizes in the next Christmas tournament at Hastings, Reshevsky being first with 7 points, Alexander and Keres equal second with 6½, and only then Flohr equal with Fine at 6 points.

Meanwhile the arrangements for his world championship match with Alekhine were going through, when suddenly the German annexation of Czechoslovakia ended everything. It must have been a sad blow, and might go to explain his bad showing in the A.V.R.O. tournament; but we must also recall that he has never scored great successes against his fellow grand masters. His speciality is beating masters who are not quite in the very top rank, and in this he is supreme. Even when scoring his greatest successes his record has been, almost monotonously, a series of wins against lower players but draws against fellow grand masters. Out of the 59 tournament games in which he has encountered the other masters who form the subject of this book, he has won but two ! Thus it was hardly surprising, when he went on to the Leningrad–Moscow tournament a few weeks later, that he staged a "come-back," finishing first, above Reshevsky and Keres, but in a field lacking any other grand master of their stamp.

HOW FLOHR PLAYS

First Illustration

The game below shows that Flohr's style had already shaped itself when he first emerged into the international limelight.

<table>
<tr><td>S. FLOHR</td><td>E. CANAL</td></tr>
<tr><td>White</td><td>Black</td></tr>
</table>

(Played in the tournament at Rogaska-Slatina, 1929.)

RUY LOPEZ

1. P–K4

Flohr likes close, or nearly close, positions, so generally avoids the P–K4 openings. As White he normally plays 1. P–Q4, 1. P–QB4, or 1. Kt–KB3; and as Black he answers 1. P–K4 by 1 . . . P–QB3, 1 . . . P–QB4, 1 . . . Kt–KB3, or 1 . . . P–K3. (He has lately taken to 1 . . . P–K4, and admitted in one article that he had handicapped himself to some extent through his limited opening repertoire.) If he opens with 1. P–K4, it is a mere formality, for even then he manages to block the game more or less.

1. . . .		P–K4
2. Kt–KB3		Kt–QB3
3. B–Kt5		P–QR3
4. B–R4		Kt–B3
5. B × Kt		

An out-of-the-way ramification of the exchange variation of the Ruy Lopez (4. B × Kt). White exchanges only after having lost a move through 4. B–R4. At first sight this appears very illogical, but in reality it is based on a well-considered plan. In the exchange variation (4. B × Kt, QP × B) 5. P–Q 4, P × P; 6. Q × P Q × Q; 7. Kt × Q is considered the strongest continuation: but this is not to Flohr's taste, because the position is too open, and because Black is left with the two Bishops for Bishop and Knight. This latter is a factor on which Flohr sets a very high valuation—he would rather play the exchange variation (that is to say, the normal line 4. B × Kt) as Black than as White.

All this does not explain the text move. Flohr knows, of course, that the Bishops are less effective in a closed position than in an open, and therefore would not permit himself to play P–Q4 or his opponent to play . . . P–KB4 in this opening, these being the very moves which would open up the position. If White, in the normal variation 4. B × Kt, QP × B, keeps the position closed by 5. Kt–B3, B–Q3 (or 5 . . . P–B3); 6. P–Q3, Black by 6 . . . Kt–K2 and an early . . . P–KB4 can ensure that his Bishops come into their own. Now, however, Black has already played . . . Kt–KB3, so that the advance . . . P–KB4 will be difficult to negotiate. Flohr has thus a reason for going over into the exchange variation, once it is certain that the position will remain, at any rate temporarily, closed.

It is worthy of note that this adapted exchange variation of Flohr's devising came into general use only five years afterwards, when Alekhine employed

it successfully in the sixteenth game of his match with
Bogolyubov in 1934.

5. . . .	QP × B
6. Kt–B3	B–QKt5
7. P–Q3	Q–K2
8. B–Q2	B–Q2
9. Kt–K2	B × Bch

This move, by which Black relinquishes the advantage of his Bishops without a struggle, is inferior.
Better 9 . . . B–Q3 followed by . . . P–B4.

10. Q × B

Threatening to win a Pawn by 11. Q–B3.

10. . . .   O–O–O

10 . . . B–Kt5 would have been better.

11. P–KR3

Forestalling . . . B–Kt5 once for all.

11. . . .   Kt–K1

Again missing the best line, 11 . . . P–B4.

12. Q–R5   P–B3

12 . . . P–QB4 was still the best.

13. P–QKt4!

Yielding White a clear positional advantage. Black's
counter-thrust . . . P–QB4 is now prevented, so that
White has a free hand in the centre. At the same time
the fixing of Black's QRP and QBP on their third rank

carries with it the permanent danger of a break-
through by P–QKt5 (preceded by P–QR4, of course).
Moves like this, which aim mainly at limiting the
mobility of the opposing pieces, are characteristic of
Flohr. It is to be noted that, after the text move,
White has difficulty in bringing his Queen back into
play. Flohr has seen clearly that he can safely permit
himself to lose a little time in this position, as his
opponent has no opportunity of opening up the game.

13.	. . .	K–Kt1
14.	Kt–Q2	Kt–Q3
15.	Q–B5	Kt–B1
16.	Q–B3	

Exchanging Queens would equalize the game completely.

16.	. . .	B–K3
17.	P–QR4	

18. P–Kt5, which Black cannot afford to allow, is
threatened already.

17.	. . .	Kt–R2
18.	P–B4!	

Strengthening his position in the centre. The ensuing exchange is practically forced.

18. . . .   P×P

19. Kt×P

Note how the preventive move 13. P–QKt4 linked up with the attacking move 18. P–B4 to eliminate all control of White's important Q4 square by a black Pawn.

19. . . .   B–B2

The more enterprising 19 . . . P–KB4 was to be considered, especially as 20. Kt×B, Q×Kt; 21. Q×KtP would be far too risky for White; but it would not have attained much because of 20. Q–K5, for instance 20 . . . KR–K1; 21. Q×B, Q×Q; 22. Kt×Q, R×Kt; 23. O–O, P×P; 24. Kt×P, after which White would have the better of it through his command of the open KB file.

20. O–O

Flohr knows little theory; he relies on experience in the main, so judges every position on its merits. This is often shown in his attitude towards castling. He does not stick to the general principle of castling as early as possible, but investigates impartially and disinterestedly whether or not it is the right move, with the result that he often gives right of way to all sorts of manœuvres before "bringing his King into safety." Only a tactician tried and tested, and immune from imaginary dangers, could attempt strategy like this.

20. . . .   R–Q2

21. KR–Kt1

Now White has suddenly obtained an excellent attacking position; the decisive break-through P–Kt5 is already on the way. Truly amazing—for White has not played for attack at all ! He has chosen a particularly peaceful variation, sacrificed nothing, and not even gone for speedy development; on the contrary, the mobilization of his pieces has proceeded with almost painful slowness. A critic imbued with classical notions of attacking play would undoubtedly disapprove of his conduct of the game; he would perhaps attempt to explain the paradox of White's obtaining the better position by some mistake on Black's part. Such a diagnosis could not content a player with modern conceptions of strategy. Between classical and modern there is here an essential difference. Formerly, people chose to employ moves aiming directly at the goal, but this method is too simple to offer real chances of success nowadays. To-day we try to camouflage our intentions as much as possible. The more we succeed in this, the more correct the strategy. It is just in this, the art of tacking about to reach one's destination, that Flohr excels. He employs moves, ostensibly quite harmless, threatening nothing, wasting time even, but in reality serving unobservedly and very gradually to create the opportunity for taking the initiative. In this game these tactics come to marvellous fruition. Admittedly Black has made one or two slightly inferior moves, but they were certainly not real mistakes.

21. . . .   **Q–K4**

By forking the white Queen and Knight, Black forces the exchange of Queens, certainly a sensible decision in view of the menacing disposition of White's pieces. As the sequel shows, however, this move has its drawbacks.

22. **Q** × **Q**   **P** × **Q**
23. **Kt–K2**

In this position White has a lot of small advantages. Firstly, the black Pawn skeleton shows weaknesses: the "doubleton" on the Bishop's file and the "single-ton" on the King's. Secondly, the white pieces are

the more effectively posted—this too as a consequence
of the Pawn situation.

In the sequel, Flohr demonstrates how excellently
he can exploit such small advantages.

23.	. . .	**R–K1**
24.	**K–B2**	**P–QKt3**
25.	**K–K3**	

White's King comes into the game without difficulty, whereas Black's must stay at home. This is the
first factor in White's advantage.

25.	. . .	**Kt–B1**
26.	**R–KB1**	**Kt–Q3**
27.	**Kt–KB3**	**K–Kt2**
28.	**P–Kt4**	**K–B1**
29.	**Kt–Kt3**	

Now White threatens to inaugurate a very dangerous
attack on the King's side, utilizing the open KB file.
What makes this attack so dangerous is the weakness
of the isolated King's Pawn, which cannot be guarded
by the Knight for the moment, so that at least one of
the black Rooks is tied down on the King's file. Correctly estimating that passive play will achieve nothing
in the long run, Black decides to counter-attack on the
opposite side.

29.	. . .	**P–B4**

Black can allow his Pawns to be doubled and isolated
because, as he has correctly foreseen, he will be able
to dissolve them again.

30.	**P×P**	**P×P**

Now the point of Black's preceding move becomes evident; if White fixes the doubled Pawns by 31. P–B4, the black Knight would travel to QB3 (via Kt2 and R4 or Q1), creating various counter-chances, among them the threat to White's Queen's Pawn. Moreover, by 31. P–B4, White would relinquish for ever the chance of playing P–Q4.

    31. **R–B2**

White ignores Black's counter-action and goes straight on with his own attack. Hence Black is practically forced to make the ensuing advance and exchange on his Q6; but after this it is not he, but his opponent, who is able to profit from the open files.

31. . . .	**P–B5**
32. **Kt–B5**	**Kt × Ktch**

32 . . . B–Kt1 was to be considered. White could have answered this by 33. R–QKt1 threatening 34. Kt × KP, R × Kt; 35. Kt × Ktch, R × Kt; 36. R–B8ch, R–Q1; 37. R–Kt8ch, K × R; 38. R × Rch, K–Kt2; 39. R × B. With the text move, Black blocks the open Bishop's file; but this means nothing, as White now obtains other open files for his Rooks.

33. **KtP × Kt**	**P × P**
34. **P × P**	**P–R3**
35. **R–B2**	

Threatening to win a Pawn by 36. R–B5, R(Q2) –K2; 37. R–R5, K–Kt2; 38. R–Kt1ch, K–R2; 39. R(Kt1)–Kt5, and 40. R × KP. Black was more or less

compelled to attempt something, but his counter-
measures on the Queen's side have only redounded to
White's advantage.

35. · · ·   **B–R4**

In order to drive away the Knight and thus, indirectly, protect the King's Pawn; but the relief is
momentary only.

36. **Kt–Q2**   **R–Q3**
37. **R–B5**!

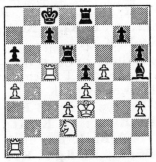

Forcing the win of Black's KP. Black cannot, with
his Bishop, simultaneously parry the threats to the
KP by the Knight from both QB4 and KB3. Nor can
he prepare to protect the Pawn further by 37 · · ·
R–Q2, because 38. Kt–B4 then threatens both 39.
Kt×P *and* 39. Kt–Kt6ch (if 38 · · · R(Q2)–K2;
39. Kt–Q6ch, winning the exchange). If 37 · · ·
R(K1)–Q1, then 38. R–R3.

37 · · · **P–Kt3**; 38. **QR–QB1, R–K2**; 39. **Kt–B4,
R–KB3**; 40. **R–B1**!

White sticks to his advantage relentlessly. The text
move needed exact calculation.

40 ... **R–Kt2;** 41. **Kt×P, P×P;** 42. **P×P, R–Kt6ch;** 43. **K–B4.**

The point of White's last move is that now 43 ... R×RP would fail through 44. R(B1)–B1, R–R5ch; 45. K–Kt3. So White maintains his material plus. It is no longer difficult to win, but it is instructive to observe how quietly and solidly Flohr winds up the affair.

43 ... **R–Kt4;** 44. **K–K4, B–K1;** 45. **Kt–Kt4, R–Q3;** 46. **P–R5, B–B3ch;** 47. **K–B4, B–Kt4;** 48. **Kt–B2, R–Kt7;** 49. **K–B3, R–Kt4;** 50. **R(B1)–B1, R–Kt2;** 51. **K–K4, R–K2ch;** 52. **R–K5, R×Rch;** 53. **K×R, K–Q1.**

53 ... B×P is refuted by 54. R–Q1; for instance, 54 ... B–Kt4; 55. R×R, P×Rch; 56. K×P, or even 56. K–B6 followed by 57. K–Kt7.

54. **P–Q4, B–B3;** 55. **R–B5, B–Kt7;** 56. **P–R4, R–Q2;** 57. **P–B6, K–K1;** 58. **Kt–Kt4, P–R4;** 59. **Kt–K3, B–B6;** 60. **R–B1, K–B2;** 61. **P–Q5, B–K7;** 62. **Kt–Kt2, B–B6;** 63. **Kt–B4, K–K1;** 64. **R–B6.**

Winning a second Pawn. Both 65. R×RP and 65. Kt–K6 are threatened.

64 ... **K–B2;** 65. **R×RP, R–Q1;** 66. **R–B6.** Black resigns.

An uncommonly good example of Flohr's style. Since his debut at Rogaska–Slatina he has won hundreds of tournament games, but few characterize his play so strikingly as this.

Second Illustration

Flohr's opponent makes a strategic mistake in the opening which might have been exploited in any of

various ways, according to style and temperament.
Let us see how Flohr goes to work to refute a strategic
error.

S. FLOHR   F. D. YATES
White   *Black*

(Played in the team tournament at Hamburg,
1930.)

QUEEN'S GAMBIT

1.	P–Q4	Kt–KB3
2.	P–QB4	P–K3
3.	QKt–B3	P–Q4
4.	B–Kt5	B–K2
5.	P–K3	QKt–Q2
6.	P×P	

Flohr was one of the first masters to make regular use
of this variation of the Queen's Gambit, and he succeeded in making it a redoubtable weapon. The text
move leads to a quiet game in which White is yet
able to preserve the advantage of the move. Something
just to Flohr's taste.

6.	. . .	P×P
7.	B–Q3	O–O
8.	Q–B2	P–B3
9.	Kt–B3	R–K1
10.	O–O	Kt–B1
11.	P–QR3	

The signal for an attack on the Queen's wing.

White is going to prepare the break-through P–QKt4 and P–Kt5.

11.	. . .	Kt–K5
12.	B×B	Q×B
13.	B×Kt	P×B
14.	Kt–Q2	B–B4

This is the mistake we mentioned. The advanced Pawn now becomes weak. 14 . . . P–KB4 should have been played. It is most interesting to see how Flohr makes full use of this opportunity and slowly gains the upper hand.

15. **P–B3**

White might have tried 15. P–B4, but with the text move he gains an important "tempo."

15. . . .   Q–Kt4

Avoiding loss of a Pawn by counter-attacking White's KP. The combination 15 . . . P×P; 16. Q×B, Q×Pch would not have been sound, because the reply 17. R–B2 would leave him with nothing more to play for.

16. **P–B4**   Q–K2

The same position would have arisen from 15. P–B4 at once, but with Black to move instead of White.

17. **Kt–K2**

Very well played. White brings his Queen's Knight to KKt3, from whence it commands both his K4 and his KB5. Black has no opportunity to carry out the manœuvre . . . B–Q2 followed by . . . P–KB4,

because, as soon as the Bishop moves, White would play
P–B5. Note that Black could offer a much stronger
resistance if White permitted him time for . . . P–KR4
and . . . P–KR5.

17. . . .	Kt–Q2
18. Kt–KKt3	Q–B3
19. Kt–B4	

White cannot capture the Pawn, of course, because
of 19 . . . Q–Kt3.

19. . . .	Kt–Kt3
20. Kt–K5	Kt–Q4
21. QR–K1	

Here 21. Kt×KP would be a mistake, because of
21 . . . Q–K2 with the double threat of 22 . . . P–B3
and 22 . . . Kt×KP. Nor could White capture the
Pawn on the next move.

21. . . .	Q–K3
22. P–R3	QR–Q1
23. Kt–R1 !	

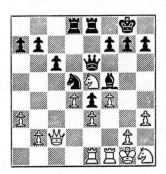

5—(G.226)

The decisive phase begins. There threatens 24. P–KKt4 and 25. P–B5, winning a piece. 23 . . . P–KR4 would allow 24. Q–K2, P–R5; 25. Q–R5, Q–B3; 26. Kt–Kt4, B×Kt; 27. P×B, and Black has no defence against the threat of 28. P–Kt5 followed by Q×RP. Flohr's manœuvring is superb. Note how Black has been continually faced with the choice between two evils: losing his King's Pawn, or leaving his Bishop in its precarious situation.

23.	. . .	**P–B3**
24.	**Kt–B4**	**B–Kt3**

Or 24 . . . P–KR4; 25. Q–K2 (25 . . . P–R5; 26. Q–R5, or 25 . . . B–Kt3; 26. P–KKt4).

25.	**P–KKt4**	**B–B2**

After 25 . . . P–KB4 White would continue his attack by Kt–Kt3, Kt–K5, etc. Nevertheless, Black would better have tried this line.

26.	**P–B5**

Compare the note to 17. Kt–K2. The isolation of the black KP is now complete.

26.	. . .	**Q–K2**
27.	**Kt–Q2**	**Kt–Kt3**
28.	**Kt–KKt3**	**B–Q4**
29.	**R–B4**	**Q–QB2**
30.	**K–B2 !**	

White could have played 30. Kt(Q2)×P; but the text move is much stronger, demonstrating peculiarly well the weakness of the KP. Black can hardly leave

this Pawn in the lurch, and has to throw several pieces
into the battle for a lost cause.

30. . . .	R–K2
31. P–KR4!	R(Q1)–K1
32. P–Kt5!	

An unusual kind of Pawn storm. After making a
long series of purely positional moves, White suddenly
develops an irresistible King's side attack. Surprising
turns like this occur frequently in Flohr's games.

32. . . .	Kt–Q2
33. R–Kt1	Q–B1
34. Kt(Kt3)×·P	

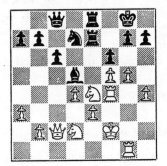

The Pawn falls at last. White has now an overwhelming position, and wins easily. It is the attack,
however, which decides the issue, and not the extra
Pawn.

34. . . .	P×P
35. P×P	Q–Kt1
36. R–Kt3	R–KB1
37. Kt–QB3.	Kt–Kt3

38. **P–B6!**	**R(K2)–KB2**
39. **Q–B5**	**Q–K1**
40. **R–R4**	

So as to force 40 ... P–Kt3, giving White a protected passed Pawn.

40. . . .	**R×P?**

A blunder in a desperate situation. Black completely overlooks the fact that White can capture twice on his KB6, thanks to his Rook on KKt3.

41. **P×R**	Resigns

This game shows that Flohr is no materialist. Notwithstanding the quietness of his style, which aims rather at gain of material than neat attack, he always thinks more of position than material, which latter he goes for only when mere positional means can carry him no farther.

Third Illustration

It is usually advantageous to retain both Bishops when your opponent has exchanged off one or both of his. Experience shows, however, that this advantage is insufficient to decide the issue in itself, as a rule. In fact it is often very far from sufficient. The ability to exploit the Bishop pair has always earned—even among famous masters—a special reputation. Of old it was Steinitz, Janovsky, and Rubinstein who possessed this reputation; nowadays Flohr is the two-Bishop king.

Here is one of his best achievements in this field—

FLOHR   BOTVINNIK
White   *Black*

(Played in the match at Moscow, 1933.)

Q.P., NIEMTSO-INDIAN DEFENCE

1. P–Q4, Kt–KB3; 2. P–QB4, P–K3; 3. QKt–B3,
B–Kt5; 4. Q–B2, P–B4; 5. P×P, Kt–R3; 6.
P–QR3, B×Ktch; 7. Q×B, Kt×P; 8. P–B3!
P–Q3; 9. P–K4, P–K4; 10. B–K3, Q–B2; 11. Kt–K2,
B–K3; 12. Q–B2, O–O; 13. Kt–B3, KR–B1; 14.
B–K2, P–QR3; 15. QR–B1, Kt(B4)–Q2; 16. Q–Q2,
Q–Kt1 (B×P? 17. Kt–Q5!); 17. Kt–Q5, B×Kt;
18. BP×B, R×Rch; 19. Q×R, Q–Q1; 20. O–O,
R–B1; 21. Q–Q2, Q–B2; 22. R–B1, Q×Rch;
23. Q×Q, R×Qch; 24. B×R.

The first part of this game does not concern us here.
We reach an end-game in which White's two Bishops
signify little, because the Pawns are split into two
equal groups, so that neither player can force a passed

Pawn. This last factor is important: the player with the two Bishops has often good winning chances if he can create a passed Pawn, whereas otherwise the most probable result is a draw. White has a little the better of the diagrammed position, for, as a result of the situation in the centre, he commands rather more of the board. Flohr avails himself of this circumstance and of his possession of the Bishop pair in impeccable fashion.

24 . . . **K–B1;** 25. **K–B2, K–K2;** 26. **B–K3, K–Q1;** 27. **K–K1, K–B2.**

Both players strive, first of all, to post their Kings as well as possible.

28. **K–Q2, Kt–QB4;** 29. **P–Q Kt4.**

Well calculated. 29 . . . Kt–R5 could now be met by 30. B–Q1, P–QKt4 (or 30 . . . *Kt–Kt3;* 31. *K–B3,* followed by 32. *P–QR4*); 31. B×Kt, P×B; 32. K–B3, K–Kt2; 33. K–B4, Kt–Q2; 34. P–Kt5, P–QR4! 35. P–Kt6, K–R3! 36. P–Kt7! Kt–Kt1 (36 . . . *K×P;* 37. K–Kt5 winning both Black's Queen's Rook's Pawns); 37. P–B4, P–B3; 38. P–B5 and Black cannot prevent the break-through by P–Kt4 and P–Kt5, as a result of which, his Pawns soon become vulnerable from the rear.

One of the chief advantages of the pair of Bishops is that their possessor can choose when to exchange.

29 . . . **Kt(B4)–Q2;** 30. **P–Kt3, Kt–Kt3;** 31. **K–B2, Kt(Kt3)–Q2.**

31 . . . Kt—R5, followed possibly by . . . P–QKt4, came rather into consideration.

32. **P–QR4, Kt–Kt3;** 33. **P–R5.**

White has decidedly strengthened his position; he

has increased his advantage in terrain, and now he can open up the Queen's side by P–Kt5 just when he likes. He wants to open up the position so as to use his Bishops actively.

With the next few moves, White goes to strengthen his position in the centre and on the Queen's wing.

33 . . . Kt(Kt3)–Q2; 34. B–QB1, K–Q1; 35. B–Kt2, Kt–K1; 36. K–Q2, Kt–B2; 37. K–K3, K–K2; 38. B–KB1, Kt–Kt4; 39. P–R4, Kt–B2; 40. B–KR3, Kt–K1; 41. P–B4! P–B3; 42. B–B5.

Forcing a slight weakening in Black's Pawn formation.

42 . . . P–KKt3; 43. B–KR3, P–R3.

So as to meet 44. P–B5 with 44 . . . P–KKt4, without allowing White to force a passed Pawn by exchanging on his Kt5. Note that this advance would have been most dangerous for Black in view of the threat of 45. P×P, P×P; 46. P–Kt4, and White obtains a passed Pawn on the King's Rook's file. Incidentally, the text move betokens a further weakening of Black's position.

44. B–QB1, Kt–Kt2; 45. P×P!

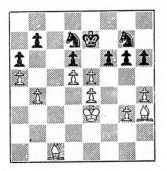

Pretty play. This gives White a protected passed
Pawn, since 45. Kt×P would fail against 46. B–B8
whilst 45. BP×P is refuted by 46. K–B3; if Black
then tries to avoid loss of a Pawn he loses a piece:
46 . . . P–R4; 47. B–Kt5ch, K–K1 (47 . . . *Kt–B3*;
48. *B–B8*); 48. B–R6!! The Knight on Kt7 has no
move, whilst the King is unable to protect both the
Knights at once. Black's next is thus forced.

A problem-like position !

45 . . . **QP×P;** 46. **K–B3, P–R4;** 47. **B–K3,
K–Q3;** 48. **B–R6, Kt–K1;** 49. **P–Kt4.**

White progresses another little step. The disappearance of two more Pawns enhances the activity
of his pieces.

49 . . . **P×Pch;** 50. **B×P, Kt–B2;** 51. **B–K3,
Kt–Kt4;** 52. **K–K2, Kt–B2;** 53. **K–Q3.**

Threatening 54. K–B4 followed by 55. B–QB5ch.
Now Black has no longer any satisfactory defence.
For instance, 53 . . . Kt–Kt4; 54. B–K6 (54. *K–B4,
Kt–R6ch*), threatening 55. B–B7.

53. . . .   **P–B4**

The only hope. Black obtains more freedom for
his pieces and eliminates the passed Pawn. Not that
this improves the situation a lot, for White obtains a
new passed Pawn on the King's Rook's file.

54. **P×P, P×P;** 55. **B×P, Kt×P;** 56. **B–Q2,
Kt(Q2)–B3;** 57. **K–B4, K–B3;** 58. **B–Kt6.**

Already the passed Pawn is threatening to advance
irresistibly.

58 . . . **P–Kt4ch;** 59. **K–Q3, Kt–K2;** 60. **B–K4ch!**

The Bishop pair is no longer the important factor.
After 60 ... Kt×B; 61. K×Kt, White would win all
the remaining black Pawns in exchange for his KRP.
The Pawn end-game after exchange of all the pieces
would be a win for him.

The remaining moves are interesting, all the same;
clearly Flohr is in no hurry to force the issue, and
plays, first of all, to win the King's Pawn.

60 **. . . Kt(K2)–Q4; 61. B–Kt5! Kt–R4.**

After 61 ... Kt×B; 62. K×Kt, Kt×P; 63. P–R5
the passed Pawn would run straight through.

62. **B–KB3, Kt–Kt6; 63. B–Q2! K–Q3;** 64.
B–Kt4, Kt–B3; 65. **B–B8, K–B3;** 66. **B–K1,
P–K5ch;** 67. **K–Q4, Kt(Kt6)–R4;** 68. **B–B5,
K–Q3;** 69. **B–Q2!**

Black resigns, as further resistance would be hopeless (69 . . . Kt–Kt6; 70. B–B4ch).

A model achievement in this type of end-game,
worthy of inclusion in every textbook.

Fourth Illustration

Flohr is first and foremost a position player, but the
next game reveals that he can also achieve excellence
in the realm of combination and attack. The essence
of his style is revealed here too: the carrying out of
preparations in an almost mysterious way. He is like
an artist roughing-in, to begin with, odd strokes and
points which seem to signify nothing; finally he links
up these random strokes—and you gaze amazed at a
perfect portrait.

FLOHR   RELLSTAB
White   *Black*

(Played in the Premier Reserves at Hastings,
1930–1.)

ENGLISH OPENING

1.	**P–QB4**	**P–QB4**
2.	**Kt–QB3**	**Kt–KB3**
3.	**P–KKt3**	**P–Q4**
4.	**P × P**	**Kt × P**
5.	**B–Kt2**	**Kt–QB2**

The continuation 5 . . . Kt × Kt and 6 . . . P–KKt3
is more usual and better.

6.	**P–Kt3**	**P–K4**

A formation considered particularly strong at the
time of this game. If Black can succeed in completing his development undisturbed, then he obtains
a positional advantage, thanks to his pressure against
White's Q4.

7.	**B–Kt2**	**B–K2**
8.	**R–B1**	

The beginning of a series of deeply conceived moves,
by which White aims, through threats on Black's BP
and KP, at destroying Black's influence in the centre.
It is to be noted that, just as in his game against
Canal, Flohr completely ignores the routine formula
"Castle early!"

8.	**. . .**	**O–O**
9.	**Kt–R4 !**	

Nor does he pay much heed to the other old maxim,
"Never move a piece twice before you have moved
every piece once." He feels that the problem of this
position is not to be solved along traditional lines.

9. . . .		Kt–Q2
10.	Kt–KB3	P–B3

This protection of the King's Pawn is quite in the
line of Black's plans.

11.	Q–B2	Kt–K3

11 . . . R–Kt1 was to be preferred, so as to be able
to play . . . P–QKt3 if necessary.

12.	Kt–R4

Compare the note to 9. Kt–R4.

12. . . .		Kt–Kt3
13.	Kt–KB5!	

Excellently played. White permits a serious weakening of his Pawn formation so as to keep his attack on
the go. After 13. Kt×Kt, P×Kt, Black's QBP would
be sufficiently protected, whereas his own QRP would
be under fire. The text move threatens 14. Kt×Bch,
followed by 15. Kt×P.

13. . . .		Kt×Kt
14.	P×Kt	R–Kt1

Preparing for P–QKt3.

15.	P–B4!

The way in which Flohr handles this game exhibits
an originality and energy which leave nothing to be

desired. The one supporting pillar in Black's position (his QBP) is far from secure even yet, and now his other centre Pawn is also under fire.

The positional text move is based on a little combination: 15 . . . P×P; 16. P×P, Kt×P; 17. Q–B4ch, Kt–K3; 18. B–Q5, K–B2 (forced), and White has now two alternative ways of regaining the sacrificed Pawn (19. Kt×P or 19. Kt×Bch). Even better chances are offered by continuing with the attack, e.g. 19. R–KKt1, P–KKt3; 20. Q–R4!, and so on.

15. . . .   P×P

Black cannot maintain his King's Pawn, for instance 15 . . . B–Q3; 16. Kt×B, Q×Kt; 17. P×P, P×P; 18. Q–K4, Kt–Q5; 19. Q–Q5ch; and White wins either the BP or the KP.

16. P×P   R–K1
17. R–KKt1 !

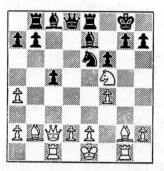

The result of White's last ten moves leaps to the eye. Black's centre has been undermined. What is still more important, White has better play for his pieces—a remarkable fact when we consider how repeatedly he has made moves directly contrary to classical rules of development. His command of the open KKt file offers him excellent attacking chances, and his superiority is really almost overwhelming. Note how safe is White's King on its original square, and how he has saved himself valuable time by foregoing castling.

| 17. . . . | B–B1 |

Clearly 17 . . . Kt×P was no longer possible (18. Q–B4ch, Kt–K3; 19. B–Q5, K–B2; 20. R×Pch or 19 . . . B–B1; 20. Kt–R6ch, K–R1; 21. Kt–B7ch and wins). But the text move too leads to forced loss. Black should have tried 17 . . . K–R1.

| 18. **B–QB6!** |

Decisive, threatening to win the exchange and also to win the Queen by Kt–R6ch and Kt–B7ch.

18. . . .	Kt–Q5
19. **Kt–R6ch**	K–R1
20. **Kt–B7ch**	K–Kt1
21. **Kt–R6ch**	

Repetition of moves to gain time.

21. . . .	K–R1
22. **Kt–B7ch**	K–Kt1
23. **Q–B4!**	

This pretty move, which threatens mate in two, required exact calculation.

23. . . .	R×Pch
24. **Q×R!**	Kt×Q
25. **Kt×Q**	Kt×R(Kt8)

Losing a piece; however 25 . . . P×B, would likewise not have sufficed to put up serious resistance, e.g. 26. K×Kt, R×B; 27. R–Kt1! R×RP (after exchange of Rooks, White would win easily); 28. R–Kt8, B–R3ch; 29. K–K3, R–R6ch; 30. K–B2, B–B5 (otherwise 31. *Kt–K6* wins); 31. P–B5! R×P; 32. Kt–K6, B×Kt; 33. P×B, R–K5; 34. R–K1 and wins. What follows now is simple.

26.	**B–Q5ch**	**K–R1**
27.	**Kt–B7ch**	**K–Kt1**
28.	**K–B2**	**Kt–R6ch**
29.	**K–Kt3**	**P–QKt4**
30.	**P×P**	**B–Kt2**
31.	**B–B4**	**P–QR3**
32.	**P–R4**	**P×P**
33.	**P×P**	**Kt×BP**
34.	**K×Kt**	**P–R4**
35.	**R–KKt1**	**K–R2**
36.	**B×P!**	

Black resigns, for, after 36 . . . P×B, he would be mated by 37. B–Q3, etc.

This magnificent game shows that Flohr's play is anything but mechanical.

Fifth Illustration

Finally, an example in which Flohr works for complications right from the beginning so as to prevent the game from becoming drawish. He reveals himself as fully up to this task, too.

M. FEIGIN   S. FLOHR
White   *Black*

(Played in the tournament at Kemeri, 1937.)

GRÜNFELD DEFENCE

1. P–Q4	Kt–KB3
2. P–QB4	P–KKt3
3. Kt–QB3	P–Q4
4. Q–Kt3	P × P
5. Q × BP	B–K3
6. Q–Kt5ch	Kt–B3
7. Kt–B3	

So far exactly as the second game in the Euwe-Alekhine match of 1935. 7. Q × P? here would allow 7 . . . Kt × P, threatening mate on the move.

7. . . .   **Kt–Q4!**

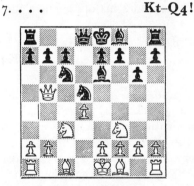

A most interesting continuation, better than the 7 . . . R–QKt1 which Alekhine played in the game cited. It has a double motive, protection (indirect) of the QKtP and prevention of White's 8. P–K4.

8. Q×P? would be answered by 8 . . . Kt(Q4)–Kt5, threatening both 9 . . . R–QKt1, winning the Queen, and 9 . . . Kt–B7ch, winning a Rook. The advance 8. P–K4 would likewise be answered by 8 . . . Kt(Q4)–Kt5 putting White into difficulties, e.g. 9. Q–R4 (9. *P–Q5, Kt–B7ch* or 9. *Q×P? R–QKt1*), 9 . . . B–Q2, 10. B–QKt5, P–QR3; 11. B×Kt, Kt×B; 12. Q–Q1, B–Kt2, and Black's two Bishops more than compensate for White's centre Pawns. One could not call 8. P–K4 a mistake, for its consequences are almost incalculable. Flohr relies mainly on getting his bearings better than his opponent in the complicated situations which would arise.

8. Kt×Kt

White wants to avoid all complications, but for this very reason concedes his opponent a most satisfactory game.

8. . . .	**B×Kt**
9. **P–K3**	**P–K3**

Demonstrating the impartiality of Flohr's judgment once again, Black has played . . . P—KKt3, the logical implication of which, as every master would agree, is the development of the KB at Kt2. Flohr sees deeper; he plays with apparent inconsistency, but it soon becomes obvious that the Bishop does better work on the diagonal KB1–QR6 than from Kt2.

A further advantage of the text move is that Black gains more influence in the centre, whilst White must take into account the possibility of . . . B×Kt followed

by . . . B–Kt5ch. This last consideration accounts for
his next move.

| | 10. **B–Q2** | **P–QR3** |

Putting an end, once for all, to the threat against
his QKtP. It is obvious that 11. Q×KtP would fail
in face of Black's 11 . . . R–R2, winning the Queen.

| | 11. **Q–R4** | **B–Q3** |

Black has already obtained a very respectable position, and he proceeds to strengthen it steadily.

	12. **B–K2**	**O–O**
	13. **Q–B2**	**Kt–Kt5**
	14. **Q–Kt1**	**P–KB4**

Preventing 15. P–K4. White's preponderance in the
centre has been definitely nullified now.

	15. **O–O**	**Kt–B3**
	16. **B–B3**	**Q–K2**
	17. **R–Q1**	

White wants to prevent or at least delay . . . P–K4.
The text move cannot be good, because White's heavy
pieces are now posted inharmoniously and hardly
efficiently. The Queen should have moved, then the
Queen's Rook. One great drawback to the text move
is that it leaves the white King inadequately protected.

| | 17. . . . | **Kt–Kt1** |

Initiating a fine cavalry manœuvre. Flohr's great
strategic abilities are exhibited markedly in this game.

| | 18. **Kt–Q2** | **Kt–Q2** |
| | 19. **B–B3** | |

Leading speedily to an exchange of the white-square Bishops, which does not improve things for White, as he is left with the "worse" Bishop (the one impeded by his own Pawns). 19. Kt–B4 would certainly have been better.

19. . . .	**Kt–B3**
20. **Q–Q3**	**Kt–K5!**

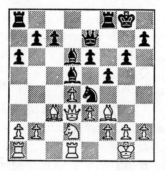

White cannot play to win a Pawn now, e.g. 21. B×Kt, P×B; 22. Kt×P, B×KRPch; 23. K×B, Q–R5ch; 24. K–Kt1, B×Kt, with a winning attack. Or 21. Kt×Kt, P×Kt; 22. B×P, B×RPch; 23. K×B, Q–R5ch; 24. K–Kt1, Q×Pch; 25. K–R2, Q–R5ch, followed by 26 . . . B×B, etc.

21. **Q–K2**   **Kt–Kt4!**

Compelling White to exchange off the white-square Bishops (disadvantageous, as already explained), for otherwise comes . . . Kt×Bch, even less pleasant.

22. **B×B**   **P×B**
23. **Kt–B3**

White ought to have made some attempt to play P–B4 followed by Kt–B3 and Kt–K5. 23. P–B4 at once would fail against 23 . . . B×P. Superior to the text move, which takes the Knight to an inferior square, would have been 23. Q–Q3.

23. . . .	Kt–K5
24. QR–B1	P–B3
25. B–K1	QR–K1
26. P–KKt3	

White tries to prevent . . . P–B5—in vain.

26. . . .	Q–Q2

Threatening 27 . . . P–B5 already (28. KtP×P, Q–Kt5ch; 29. K–B1 or K–R1, B×P; 30. P×B, Kt–Kt6ch, etc.).

27. Q–B1	P–KKt4
28. R–Q3	P–B5

Black's preparations have been masterly, and with the text move he embarks on the decisive attack. White is in an untenable situation.

29. KP×P	P×P
30. Kt–R4	B–K2
31. Kt–B3	B–Q3

As in the last game, a repetition of moves to gain time.

32. Kt–R4	K–R1
33. Q–Kt2	P×P
34. RP×P	Kt–Kt4
35. P–B3	

Producing weaknesses, but no other move would save the situation. For instance, 35. K–R2 would be refuted by 35 . . . Q–Kt5 with 36 . . . Q×Ktch in prospect.

35. · · ·		**Kt–R6ch**
36. **K–R1**		

Not to R2, because of 36 . . . Kt–B5!; 37. P×Kt, B×Pch and wins.

36. · · ·		**B–K2!**

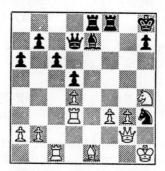

The white Knight having no square of retreat, a new weakening of the castled position is inevitable; further resistance is then out of the question. It should be noted that 37. K–R2 is useless on account of 37 . . . B×Kt; 38. Q×Kt? R–K7ch, winning the Queen.

37. **B–Q2**	**B×Kt**
38. **P×B**	**Q–B4**
39. **R–Kt3**	**R–KKt1**
40. **Q–R2**	**R–K3**
41. **R–B1**	

Enabling Black to clinch the issue outright, the
Rook's station at B1 being accidentally unfortunate.

41. . . .   **Kt–B7ch!**

A pretty concluding stroke. The Knight must be
taken, and after either 42. R × Kt, Q–Kt8ch or
42. Q × Kt, Q–R6ch, White is mated. With this
beautiful game we say good-bye to Flohr and pass on
to the leading representative in master chess of the
Union of Soviet Socialist Republics.

CHAPTER V
MICHAEL MOISIAYOVITCH BOTVINNIK

M. Botvinnik was born on 11th April, 1911, some-where in Russia; to judge by his name, probably in the Ukraine. For as long as he has been known as a chess player, he has lived in Leningrad. He studied physics and graduated as an electrical engineer. It was in 1924 that he learnt chess, and his rare gift became immediately apparent. As early as 1926 he was permitted to compete in the championship of Leningrad, finishing second. In 1927 he was recognized officially as a Soviet master, after having attained fifth place in the national championship and won first prize in a Leningrad tournament. He repeated this latter success in 1930, and has regularly competed in all the important Russian events ever since. He became a professional player—a career which in Russia implies a Civil Service status. A year later, in 1931, he won the championships not only of Leningrad (winning 12 games, losing 1 and drawing 4) but also of the whole Soviet Union (18 wins, 4 losses, 4 draws), and since then has remained the unchallenged leader of Soviet chess. That Levenfish held the actual title for a while was a mere formality: Botvinnik did not take part in the championship tournament of 1937, but it was arranged that whoever won this tournament should play a match against him to decide the championship for that year. Thus there came about a match between Botvinnik and Levenfish in which, to the surprise of the whole world, Levenfish succeeded in

MICHAEL MOISIAYOVITCH BOTVINNIK
Primarily a position player, but brilliant in attack

holding his own (the match being drawn) and consequently remained in possession of the title. Whilst
cordially congratulating Levenfish on his achievement,
one must regard as purely formal an arrangement
through which Botvinnik was deprived of his title
without being defeated. So much for the domestic side
of Botvinnik's career.

In the inter-city match Stockholm–Leningrad, held
in the Swedish capital in 1929, he defeated Stoltz. His
second encounter with a foreigner of any consequence
came towards the end of 1933, when by drawing his
match against Flohr (2 wins, 8 draws 2 losses,) he
qualified as an international great master with honours.

Now the whole chess world was anxious to see him
playing in a tournament with leading non-Russian
masters, preferably outside the U.S.S.R. The tournament of twelve in Leningrad (August, 1934), which he
won, hardly satisfied these desires, for only two
foreigners, Euwe and Kmoch, took part. His participa-
tion in the Hastings tournament of 1934–5 aroused
eager anticipation, the more so as this tournament was
particularly strongly contested, the four other visiting
masters being none other than Capablanca, Flohr,
Lilienthal, and Euwe. The result of this first excursion
into the outer world was a bitter disappointment—he
came fifth. Had "Europa" (as the Soviets call Europe
outside of their own land) overvalued him? The
cognoscenti could not believe it, and events justified
them. On 14th February, only a few weeks later,
there started an international tournament at Moscow,
comprising eight visiting grand masters and twelve of
the strongest Russians. Botvinnik forged ahead, to tie

for ultimate first place with Flohr. The quality of this success can be gauged through a survey of the results of the other visiting great masters. Lasker came third, Capablanca fourth, Spielmann fifth, Lilienthal eighth; Stahlberg sixteenth, Pirc eighteenth, and Miss Menchik in last place. This result impelled the Russian chess organizers (an official body) to announce a double-round tournament of ten players a year later, the five best Russian players matching their prowess with five leading foreign masters. In this tournament, which commenced on 14th May, 1936, Botvinnik fully upheld his reputation, as the score card shows: Capablanca 13, Botvinnik 12, Flohr 9½, Lilienthal 9, Ragozin 8½, Lasker 8, Eliskases, Kahn, Levenfish and Riumin all equal 7½.

The fact that Botvinnik had scored all his great successes in his own country, whereas his only appearance abroad had been a disappointment, rendered it highly desirable for his reputation that he should, at any rate on one occasion, attain his best overseas. The Nottingham tournament gave him this opportunity, which he seized with both hands. His victory, in company with Capablanca, was gained in handsome style.

In the A.V.R.O. tournament he played superbly steady chess; after losing in the first round to Fine he climbed, by the eleventh round to second place. Then he relaxed, blundering badly in a perfectly innocuous position against Euwe and frittering away an overpowering advantage against Flohr. Third to Keres and Fine in the final table, he could yet look back on his performance not without satisfaction.

A few months later he retained his Soviet championship at Moscow, making no mistake in a crucial final round.

By all these magnificent achievements Botvinnik has gained an assured place within the small circle of grand masters who may be regarded as serious contenders for the world-championship throne.

BOTVINNIK MAKES HIS BOW
First Illustration

One of the openings which Botvinnik likes to adopt is the Sicilian Defence. This is one of the most difficult of openings, there being little chance of its leading to a drawn position at any early stage. White gets more terrain and various attacking possibilities. Black, on the other hand, entrenches himself behind a sort of "Maginot Line," ready at any time for a sudden counter-attack; for this he needs the utmost self-reliance, otherwise the chances may turn definitely against him. An opening which allows Botvinnik to exploit his curious abilities to the full. Here is a beautiful example—

V. A. ROUZER   M. M. BOTVINNIK
White   *Black*

(Played in the Leningrad tournament, 1933.)

SICILIAN DEFENCE

1. P–K4, P–QB4; 2. Kt–KB3, Kt–QB3; 3. P–Q4, P×P; 4. Kt×P, Kt–KB3; 5. Kt–QB3, P–Q3; 6. B–K2, P–KKt3; 7. B–K3, B–Kt2; 8. Kt–Kt3, B–K3; 9. P–B4, O–O; 10. O–O.

For some time the lively 10. P–Kt4 was regarded as

strongest; the game we give next, Alekhine *v.* Botvinnik, modified this opinion, however.

       10. . . .   **Kt–QR4**
       11. **Kt×Kt**

According to current ideas, which are based on
study of numerous games opened like this, the most
promising continuation here is 11. P–B5, B–B5;
12. B–Q3.

       11 . . . **Q×Kt;** 12. **B–B3, B–B5;** 13. **R–K1,**
KR–Q1; 14. **Q–Q2, Q–B2.**

Black retires his Queen so as not to have continually to reckon with the possibility of Kt–Q5. This
manœuvre might be very troublesome, though there
would be nothing in it at the moment (15. Kt–Q5,
Q×Q; 16. B×Q, Kt×Kt; 17. P×Kt, B×KtP,
etc.).

The position we have reached is characteristic of
the Sicilian. White commands more of the board and
must strive to post his Knight on Q5; should he succeed, then he would have much the better game.
In practice, he rarely does.

       15. **QR–B1**

White wants to play P–QKt3, preparing P–QB4.

       15. . . .   **P–K4!**

A strong and, as soon appears, deeply calculated
move.

       16. **P—QKt3**

White plays to a consistent plan. This move safeguards his QKtP and envisages an eventual Kt–Q5.

16. Kt–Q5 at once would lose a Pawn through
16 . . . Kt×Kt; 17. P×Kt, P×P; 18. B×BP,
B×KtP or 18. B–Q4, B–K4.

16. P×P was playable: 16 . . . P×P; 17. Q–B2;
but then Black would have a thoroughly satisfactory
game.

16. . . .   **P–Q4!!**

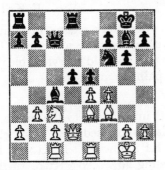

A splendid and totally unexpected continuation,
Black making a sudden sharp attack. Pure Botvinnik !

17. **KP×P**

White was faced with an unpleasant choice, as the
following analyses reveal—

(a) 17. P×B, P×P recovering the piece with a fine
game;

(b) 17. Kt×P, B×Kt; 18. P×B, P–K5; 19. B–K2,
Kt×P with a clear advantage;

(c) 17. BP×P, Kt×P; 18. B×Kt, P×B; 19.
Q–B2, B×KP, and Black wins White's KRP. This
last variation yields White plenty of counter-chances,
all the same; e.g. 20. Kt×P, B×Pch; 21. K–R1,

B–K3; 22. Kt–B6ch (22. *P–Kt3, B–Q4!*), 22 . . . K–R1;
23. B–Q4, and now it is White who has the best of it.
But Black need not go for the Pawn. (19 . . .
Q×K P looks a stronger alternative.—*Translators*.)

After the text move White is up against a much more
difficult task, the manifold ingenuities of Botvinnik's
combination being fully revealed.

17. . . .   P–K5!

By this Pawn offer Black secures maximum freedom
for his pieces without wasting any time. To retire his
attacked Bishop to R3 would lose valuable time, and he
is at particular pains to avoid that.

18. P × B

White submits unwillingly to the indirect exchange
of his KB for Black's exposed QB. What else could he
do? On 18. B × KP follows 18 . . . Kt × B; 19. Kt × Kt,
B × QP, threatening 20 . . . B × Kt or (if the attacked
Knight should move away) 20 . . . B–B6 winning the exchange, so that White is forced to play 20. Q–Q3; then
his KKtP is lost: 20 . . . Q–B3! 21. B–B2, P–B4, etc.

Another possibility was 18. Kt × P, Kt × P (threatening 19 . . . *Kt × B* followed by 20 . . . *B–Q5* winning
the Queen); 19. K–R1, Kt × B; 20. Q × Kt, and
Black has a fine game; though whether he could play
to win the exchange by 20 . . . B–Q5; 21. Q–Q2,
B–Kt7 is doubtful; for instance 22. Q–Kt4, B × R;
23. Kt–B6ch, K–R1; 24. Q–B3, B–Q7; 25. Q–Kt2,
B–K3 (25 . . . *Q–Q3?*; 26. *R–K8ch!* and wins); 26.
Kt–Q5ch, B–B6; 27. Kt × B, K–Kt1; 28. Kt–K4,
Q × KBP; 29. Kt–B6ch, K–B1; 30. Kt × Pch and the
win (for Black) is problematical.

Finally, 18. B–K2 would lead (after 18 . . . B × QP) to the same sorts of position as arise from 17. Kt × P (see the note to 17. KP × P).

18. . . .   **P × B**
19. **P–QB5**

White's two advanced Pawns look dangerous, but the other side of the picture is soon seen. His position is too loose; his Pawns and pieces co-operate awkwardly, consequently Black continually finds new points to attack. Notice the important part played by the black Pawn on B6.

19. . . .   **Q–R4!**

A very strong move. The main threat is 20 . . . Kt–Kt5, after which 21. B–Q4 would fail in face of 21 . . . P–B7ch or 21 . . . B × Bch followed by 22 . . . P–B7ch, winning a Rook. Any move of the attacked Knight would lose likewise, e.g. 21. Kt–Kt1, Q × Q; 22. Kt × Q (22. *B × Q, P–B7ch*), 22 . . . Kt × B; 23. R × Kt, B–Q5, and so on. The refutation of 21. Kt–K4 (after 20 . . . Kt–Kt5) is also pretty: 21 . . . Q × Q; 22. B × Q, P–B7ch; 23. Kt × P, B–Q5 winning the exchange and several Pawns.

Apart from 20 . . . Kt–Kt5 there threatens 20 . . . Kt × P; 21. Kt × Kt, Q × Q; 22. B × Q, R × Kt, and White is lost in view of the innumerable weaknesses in his Pawn position. Nevertheless, White could have put up a more extended resistance in this way, and therefore 20. P × P would have been best on the whole, getting rid of "public enemy No. B3."

Yet another move worth considering was 20. Q–Q3,

e.g. 20 . . . Kt–Kt5; 21. Kt–K4. But then 21 . . .
P–B4 would be extremely strong (22. Kt–Q6? P–B7ch;
23. B×P, Kt×B; 24. K×Kt, Q×BPch, winning a
piece).

20. KR–Q1

With the idea of further protecting the Queen's
Pawn, and also ruling out all eventualities in which
Black threatened the Rook by . . . P–B7ch. Black's
attack, however, is becoming irresistible, thanks to the
pin on White's Knight and the co-operation of the
advanced KBP. Some beautiful operations follow.

20. . . .   **Kt–Kt5**

There is no adequate defence to this move. The best
of a bad job would be 21. Kt–K4, Q×Q; 22. B×Q,
B–Q5ch; 23. K–R1 (forced), 23 . . . P×Pch; 24.
K×P, R×P; but this would lead to an end-game in
which White has no fewer than five isolated Pawns.

21. B–Q4

This is the move which White had in mind when he

played 20. KR–Q1; now he need not capture the
KBP when it advances.

21. ...	**P–B7ch!**
22. **K–B1**	

Forced; the King cannot go to R1 because of
22 . . . R×P; 23. Kt×R (or 23. *Kt–K2*) 23 . . . P–B8
(Queens) ch! 24. R×Q, Q×Q and wins. Apparently
White overlooked this pretty finesse until too late,
otherwise he would have captured the Pawn. On B1
the white King is very unsafe, as Botvinnik reveals by
a series of powerful strokes.

22. ...	**Q–R3ch!**
23. **Q–K2**	

Again forced. There was no interposing the Knight,
e.g. 23. Kt–K2, R×P; 24. P–B3, R–K1; or 24.
P–B4, B×B (threatening mate); 25. Kt×B, QR–Q1;
26. Q–B3, Q×RP (threatening mate again); 27.
R–B2 (or 27. R–Q2), 27. . . R×Kt! and Black has
a won game, in view of the chances of promoting his
Pawn. 23. Q–Q3 would also lose by force, through
23 . . . B×B; 24. Q×Q, Kt–K6ch; 25. K–K2,
P–B8 (Queens) ch! 26. R×Q, P×Q and Black has
won a piece.

23. ...	**B×B**
24. **R×B**	

Exchanging Queens would again lose a piece by
24 . . . Kt–K6ch.

24. ...	**Q–KB3**

The black Queen suddenly takes over a decisive role

on the King's wing, gaining valuable time by attacking
the undefended Rook.

> 25. **R(B1)–Q1**

25. Q–Q2 would be just as hopeless: 25 . . . Q–R5;
or 25. Q–Q3, R–K1; 26. P–KR3, Q–R5.

> 25. . . .   **Q–R5**
> 26. **Q–Q3**   **R–K1**

With two mating threats, viz. 27 . . . Kt×P and
27 . . . R–K8.

> 27. **R–K4**   **P–B4!**
> 28. **R–K6**

Exchanging Rooks would rob the white King of its
only remaining flight square, and allow 28. (R×Rch)
R×R; 29. Q–Kt3, Kt×Pch; 30. K×P, Kt–Kt5ch;
31. K–B3, R–K6 mate.

> 28. . . .   **Kt×Pch**
> 29. **K–K2**   **Q×P!**

And now Black threatens to win a whole Rook by
queening the Pawn. The only plausible reply, 30.

R–KB1, would allow Black to appropriate the exchange by 30 . . . R×Rch and 31. Kt×R, and he would then have enough for a win. He has an even stronger resource, 30 . . . QR–Q1!, and against the threat of winning a whole Rook (by 31. . . R×R) which this introduces there is no resource whatever, e.g. 31. R×BP, Q–KKt5ch, etc. Or 31. R×Rch, R×Rch, etc. Or finally 31. R–K3, Kt×R.

So White resigns.

A grand achievement which gained a well-deserved brilliancy prize.

Second Illustration

Next, a game with the same opening but in which White selects the most violent treatment; moreover, it is Alekhine who plays White, a guarantee that every chance of attack will be energetically seized. Nevertheless, Botvinnik manages to keep the balance; the more vigorously he is attacked, the sharper are his counter-measures. The outcome is a superb draw.

DR. A. ALEKHINE   M. M. BOTVINNIK
White   *Black*

(Played in the Nottingham tournament, 1936.)

SICILIAN DEFENCE

1. P–K4, P–QB4; 2. Kt–KB3, P–Q3; 3. P–Q4, P×P; 4. Kt×P, Kt–KB3; 5. Kt–QB3, P–KKt3; 6. B–K2, B–Kt2; 7. B–K3, Kt–B3; 8. Kt–Kt3, B–K3; 9. P–B4, O–O; 10. P–Kt4.

Threatening 11. P–Kt5, which would drive away Black's KKt and diminish his influence in the centre. Unless he is to be hemmed in, Black must engineer a counter-action immediately. A very difficult task here, which, however, Botvinnik fulfils immaculately.

10. . . .   **P–Q4!!**

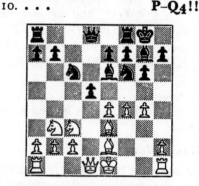

This thrust is positionally justified in every way, but it is extraordinarily difficult to work out all its thorny tactical consequences. Brilliancies ensue.

11. **P–B5**

If 11. P–K5, then 11 . . . Kt–K1 or (certainly keener) 11 . . . P–Q5! 12. P×Kt, B×BP!, regaining the piece with a good game; or 11 . . . P–Q5; 12. Kt×P, Kt×Kt; 13. B×Kt (13. *P×Kt, B×BP!*) 13 . . . Kt×P! (14. B×Kt, B×B; 15. Q×B, Q×B) with the same result.

11. . . .   **B–B1!**

In such an involved position it is curious that Black should be able to permit himself such a meek retreat, but any other move would lead him into serious trouble. Botvinnik has foreseen well that the loss of time involved does not impair the effectiveness of his counter-attack. 11. P–B5 has weakened White's position in the centre; he can no longer play P–K5.

12. **KP × P**

Clearly enough, White has nothing better.

12. . . .   **Kt–Kt5**

Threatening to capture the Queen's Pawn with either Knight, or alternatively 13 . . . P × P; for instance, 13. B–B3, P × P; 14. P–QR3, P × P, etc.

13. P × P, RP × P; 14. B–B3 would now set Black a difficult problem. White's plus Pawn on Q5 is now adequately protected, whilst 15. P–QR3 threatens. If the black Knight be then forced to withdraw to QR3, White has a won game at once. It would therefore be up to Black to find some way of keeping his action on the go; a passive move would spell certain downfall. Such a continuation indeed exists, namely (13. P × P, RP × P; 14. B–B3), Kt × KtP!! 15. B × Kt, B × B; 16. Q × B, B × Ktch; 17. P × B, Kt × BPch; 18. K–K2, Kt × R; 19. R × Kt, Q × P and, White's position is torn to shreds, apart from the fact that, with a Rook and two Pawns for two minor pieces, Black might consider himself materially to the good as well.

13. **P–Q6!**

Very strongly played. The main threat is 14. P–QR3, the secondary 14. P × KP, Q × P; 15. B–B5. Black must not now play 13 . . . KP × P because of 14. P–QR3 followed by 15. P–Kt5 and 16. P–B6. So the next move is forced.

13. . . .   **Q × P**
14. **B–B5**

The point of White's counter-sacrifice. After 14 . . .
Q×Qch; 15. R×Q! Kt–B3 (15 . . . *Kt×BPch*; 16.
K–Q2, P–Kt3; 17. *B×KP* and wins) White would
definitely take the lead. Note that 14. Q×Q would be
weak because Black, after recapturing, would have the
threats 15. Kt×BPch and 15 . . . P×P at his disposal.

14. . . .   Q–B5!

Based on the consideration that, if the exchange of
Queens can be avoided, the exposed situation of the
white King must become the crucial factor. Black has
a drawing line up his sleeve, too, in the event of his
opponent's going for the win of a piece.

15. KR–B1

White, realizing that the exposed situation of his
King would compromise any attempt to intensify the
struggle, lets Black go through with his drawing
combination.

15. . . .   Q×RP!
16. B×Kt   Kt×P!

The whole point ! 17 . . . Q–Kt6ch is now threatened;
18. K–Q2, B–R3ch, with mate to follow. White must
accept the second sacrifice.

17.	**B×Kt**	**Q–Kt6ch**
18.	**R–B2**	

Once again forced, for 18. K–K2?, Q×Bch; or 18.
K–Q2, B–R3ch would lose quickly.

18.	**. . .**	**Q–Kt8ch**
19.	**R–B1**	

White can never move his King. The text move
reveals the significance of 16 . . . Kt×P!, for White
cannot interpose his Bishop on B1 now. Thus perpetual
cneck, by Q–Kt6–Kt8, is inescapable.

A most pleasant drawn game, brief yet rich in
combination. It is characteristic of both adversaries,
each a connoisseur in the creative, efficient, and aggressive handling of the openings, that the struggle was
sharp from the very outset.

Third Illustration

One of Botvinnik's principal characteristics, which
he shares with some of the other prominent masters
of the younger generation, is great patience. If there
are neither possible combinations nor objects of immediate attack, he knows how to manœuvre, tack about,
and slowly improve his position, utilizing every little
opportunity.

Here is an example.

M. M. BOTVINNIK   S. FLOHR
White   *Black*

(Played in the tournament at Moscow, 1936.)

ALEKHINE'S DEFENCE

1. **P–K4, Kt–KB3;** 2. **P–K5, Kt–Q4;** 3. **P–Q4, P–Q3;** 4. **Kt–KB3, B–Kt5;** 5. **B–K2, P–QB3;** 6. **O–O, P×P.**

Another game, played between the same opponents three months later in Nottingham, went as follows: 6 . . . B×Kt!; 7. B×B, P×P; 8. P×P, P–K3; 9. Q–K2, Q–B2; 10. P–B4, Kt–K2!; 11. B–Kt4, Kt–Q2; 12. P–B4, P–KR4; 13. B–R3, O–O–O; 14. B–K3, Kt–KB4; 15. B×Kt, P×B; 16. Q–KB2, Q–R4; perfectly satisfactorily for Black. (17. B×P? P–QKt3 !) The move played here is not so good.

7. **Kt×P!**   **B×B**
8. **Q×B**

The distinction between the two continuations 6 . . . B×Kt! and 6 . . . P×P lies in the resulting central formation of White's Pawns: in the one case his QP goes to K5, in the other it remains on Q4. The latter formation provides the better chances, since it is more dynamic, the square K5 remaining open for the use of the white pieces.

8 . . . **Kt–Q2;** 9. **P–KB4, P–K3;** 10. **P–B4, Kt(Q4)–Kt3;** 11. **B–K3, B–K2;** 12. **Kt–QB3, O–O.**

Black commands much too little of the board, and must defend carefully—a task which Flohr tackles very well indeed. A hard fight ensues in which Botvinnik manages to turn his superior mobility to account.

13. **R–B3**

The "natural" continuation was 13. QR–Q1, but

the text move is stronger, threatening 14. R–R3 followed by Q–R5, and compelling Black to take immediate counter-measures.

13. . . .   **Q–K1**

So as to answer 14. R–R3 with 14 . . . P–KB4 and nip White's King's side attack in the bud.

14. **R–Q1**

14. R–R3 would now be mere waste of time.

14. . . .   **R–Q1**
15. **P–QKt3**   **P–KB4**

Now necessary; Black has to strive for some grip on the centre so as to be able to manœuvre more easily. The text move creates a backward Pawn on his K3 which, whilst it has no immediate significance, makes its presence felt: throughout all possible simplifications Flohr must take care to insure against its suddenly becoming weak, as would happen, for instance, if he were to advance his QBP and permit QP×QBP. The text move makes Black's position more rigid and robs it of some of its flexibility.

16. **Kt–Q3**

The first of a series of moves by which White does nothing but emphasize his superior mobility. Above all, to achieve this, he avoids exchanges.

16. . . . **B–B3;** 17. **B–B2, Q–B2;** 18. **Kt–K1, KR–K1;** 19. **R(B3)–Q3, Kt–KB1;** 20. **Kt–B3, Q–B2;** 21. **Kt–K5.**

According to Botvinnik, 21. P–Kt3 was preferable, protecting the KBP and still further facilitating White's manœuvring.

21. . . .	Kt(Kt3)–Q2
22. Q–Q2	B–K2
23. Kt–B3	

Compare the note to White's sixteenth move. This moving to and fro of the Knight seems bad, but we can hardly speak here of loss of time. The essential criterion of a loss of time, that the other side should be able to profit by it, is missing. Botvinnik manœuvres profoundly, strengthening his position bit by bit; for instance the doubling of his Rooks was a step forward.

23. . . .	Kt–B3
24. Q–B1!	

Prudent play. Black threatened 24 . . . B–Kt5 followed by 25 . . . Kt–K5, or by 25 . . . B × Kt and 26 . . . Kt–K5, after which the Knight could be dislodged from its advanced post only with difficulty. White by the text move avoids this simplification. Botvinnik plans to reply to 24 . . . B–Kt5 with 25. Kt–Kt1 !, subsequently driving away the Bishop. Then his Queen's Knight could return to QB3 and carry out its duty of keeping an eye on K4.

24. . . .	Kt–K5
25. Kt–K5	Kt × B

25 . . . Kt × Kt would have been a little better. The removal of the Knight on White's QB3 would have

given Black the chance to establish his second Knight on K5.

26.	**K × Kt**	**Kt–Q2**
27.	**Q–K3**	**Kt × Kt**

This exchange serves to close the King's file for White and bring Black's backward King's Pawn into safety, but it carries another danger in its trail; White's central formation is strengthened and Black has a positional weakness at his Q3, whose significance is speedily revealed.

28.	**BP × Kt**	**Q–R4**

Aiming to exchange off the white Knight by 29 . . . B–Kt5. This move would not have been possible without the preceding exchange, because of the reply Kt × Kt, followed by Q × Pch.

29.	**P–QR4**

Safeguarding the QRP so that 29 . . . B–Kt5 could now be met simply by moving away the attacked Knight.

29 . . . **R–Q2**; 30. **P–Kt3, Q–Q1**; 31. **K–Kt2, B–Kt4**; 32. **Q–B3, Q–K2**; 33. **P–B5!**

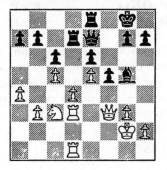

After this advance, White suddenly has a positional superiority. Whereas, up to now, the position has been in White's favour only in a general way, his advantage now takes tangible form. There is a direct threat of Kt–Kt1–R3–B4–Q6, followed by P–QKt4–Kt5, against which Black can do little.

33. · · ·   **P–QR4**

Black cannot prevent the Knight manœuvre, but he can stop the Pawn push. If the white QKtP advances now, Black will exchange it off.

This resource is not completely satisfactory, as White can, sooner or later, employ P–QKt4 to open up the QKt file for his own benefit.

34. **Kt–Kt1, Q–B1 ; 35. Kt–R3, B–Q1 ; 36. Kt–B4, B–B2 ; 37. Kt–Q6, R–Kt1 ; 38. R–QKt1.**

Another very attractive possibility was the sacrificial line 38. Kt × KtP, R × Kt, 39. Q × QBP followed by 40. Q × Pch. But Botvinnik is not keen on combinations without a clear aim. If he has the better of it, then he tries to avoid complications.

38. · · ·	**Q–Q1**
39. **P–QKt4**	**P × P**
40. **R × P**	**B × Kt**

White could attack the QKtP four times over, whereas Black can defend it only thrice. Consequently the exchange in the text is quite unavoidable, and might have had to be carried out under even more unfavourable circumstances if postponed. White has now a very strong passed Pawn, whilst the King's file is opened up once again.

41. **KP×B**   **Q–R4**
42. **R(Q3)–Kt3**   **R–K1**

So as to get chances of perpetual check after 43.
R×P, R×R; 44. R×R, Q×RP; the white King
being somewhat insecurely situated. But White fights
shy of all double-edged possibilities.

43. **Q–K2**   **Q–R1**
44. **R–K3**   **K–B2**
45. **Q–B4**

45. K–R3 or K–Kt1 would have been more solid.
The text allows Black to stage an apparent surprise, but
White is well prepared.

45. . . .   **P–QKt4!**

A pretty stroke. White cannot capture the courageous
Pawn, for 46. RP×P?? would lose the Queen (46 . . .
P×Pch), whilst it is doubtful whether White's two
passed Pawns would be a lot of use after 46. P×Pe.p.,
P–B4ch; 47. P–Kt7, R×KtP; 48. R×R, Q×Rch;
49. K–R3, P×P.

46. **Q–B2**

Holding on to his advantage; he now threatens
47. P×P.

46. . . .   **R×P?**

This violent attempt to profit from the momentarily
unsheltered situation of the white King loses by force.
46 . . . P×P would have been better; it is doubtful

whether Black could hold out indefinitely in any case,
however.

47.	**P × R**	**P–B4ch**
48.	**K–R3**	**P × R**
49.	**Q–B7ch**	**K–Kt1**
50.	**P–Q7**	

The move 46 . . . R × P smashed the position completely open, allowing White to penetrate with his
Queen and capitalize his passed Queen's Pawn. The
win is no longer difficult.

50.	**. . .**	**R–KB1**

If 50 . . . R–Q1, then 51. R × P (threatening Q × R !),
K–B2; 52. Q–Q6 and wins.

51.	**Q–Q6**	

Another winning line was 51. R × P. The text move
threatens to finish the game at once by 52. Q × Pch,
K–R1; 53. Q–K8.

51.	**. . .**	**P–R3**
52.	**Q × Pch**	**K–R2**
53.	**Q–K8**	**P–Kt6**

Black tries a little trap. Now 54. Q×Q, R×Q; 55. R–K8 would be answered by 55 . . . P–Kt7; 56. R×R, P–Kt8(Q), 57. P–Q8 (Q)? (57. R–R8ch is correct), 57 . . . Q–KB8ch; 58. K–R4, P–Kt4ch mating or winning the Queen.

54.	Q×Q	R×Q
55.	P×P	R–Q1
56.	R×P	R×P
57.	P–Kt6	. . .

The game was adjourned here, and Black resigned without further play.

No spectacular, but yet a very good, achievement. Botvinnik held fast to his opening advantage and increased it so remorselessly that his opponent was finally driven to a despairing counter-attack which only precipitated the end.

Fourth Illustration

Finally, a brilliant example of Botvinnik's attacking power.

M. M. BOTVINNIK   V. A. CHEKOVER
White   *Black*

(Played in the Moscow tournament, 1935.)

RETI SYSTEM

1. Kt–KB3, P–Q4; 2. P–B4, P–K3; 3. P–QKt3, Kt–KB3; 4. B–Kt2, B–K2; 5. P–K3, O–O; 6. B–K2.

Niemtzovitsch used to handle this opening rather differently, postponing P–QB4 or omitting it altogether and playing Kt–K5, followed by P–KB4 as

early as possible. A downright plan like this is not to
Botvinnik's taste. He prefers to adopt a more reserved
attitude, consistently with his predilection for attacks
which savour rather of counter-thrusts.

| 6. . . . | **P–B3** |

6 . . . P–B4, followed by . . . Kt–B3, was to be
preferred.

7. **O–O**	**QKt–Q2**
8. **Kt–B3**	**P–QR3**
9. **Kt–Q4**	

A characteristic move. White does not want to
transpose into the Queen's Gambit by 9. P–Q4, for
this would make the position less complicated. So he
plans to go through with Niemtsovitch's idea (by P–B4,
followed by Kt–B3 and Kt–K5). At the same time he
tempts Black to weaken his centre by . . . P–K4 (which
would be answered by Kt–B5) or . . . P–B4, which,
though objectively not unfavourable for Black, would
set him some difficult problems after the reply Kt–B2
(or even Kt–B3), producing a position of a type that
suits Botvinnik particularly well.

| 9. . . . | **P×P** |

This surrender of the centre is bad. Black wants to
play . . . P–K4 with gain of time; the plan goes
wrong, however, with the result that White obtains a
clear superiority in the centre.

| 10. **P×P** | **Kt–B4** |
| 11. **P–B4** | |

Parrying the positional threat of 11 . . . P–K4,
12. Kt–B3, Kt–Q6.

11. . . .	Q–B2
12. **Kt–B3**	**R–Q1**
13. **Q–B2**	

The final preparation for the advance of the QP.
If 13. P–Q4 at once, 13 . . . QKt–K5 forces off one
minor piece on each side, to lighten Black's task
slightly.

13 . . . **Kt(B4)–Q2**; 14. **P–Q4, P–B4**; 15. **Kt–K5,
P–QKt3**; 16. **B–Q3, P×P**; 17. **P×P, B–Kt2**;
18. **Q–K2, Kt–B1.**

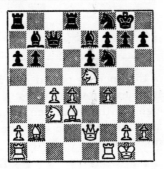

A very familiar type of position has been reached.
White has "hanging" Pawns at Q4 and QB4 and is
more or less compelled to play for a King's side attack,
which has, however, under the circumstances, every
chance of succeeding. White usually works for P–Q5
or P–KB5 in such positions. Botvinnik tackles the
problem in an altogether different way: he brings his

QKt over to the King's wing, where it decisively strengthens the attack. Each of his next few moves deserves an exclamation mark.

        19. **Kt–Q1**   **R–R2**
        20. **Kt–B2**   **Q–Kt1**
        21. **Kt–R3**   **P–R3**
        22. **Kt–Kt5 !**

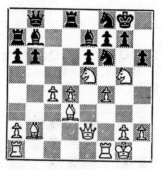

The piano of the opening passed into a crescendo in the middle-game and now becomes a fortissimo of attack. Throughout the next ten moves sacrificial combinations are always in the air; the black King's stronghold is smashed open with titanic power.

        22. . . .   **P × Kt**

There is no choice; any other move would lose to 23. Kt(Kt5) × BP.

        23. **P × P**   **Kt(B1)–Q2**

If 23 . . . Kt(B3)–Q2, then 24. Kt × P wins.

        24. **Kt × P !**

Beautifully played. There were other good continuations here, but White consistently finds the strongest.

24. . . .	**K × Kt**
25. **P–Kt6ch**	**K–Kt1**

25 . . . K–K1 or K–B1 would permit White an ample choice of winning continuation, e.g.—

(a) 25 . . . K–B1; 26. Q × P, Kt–K4; 27. P × Kt or more prettily 27. R × Ktch, P × R (27 . . . *B × R*, 28. *B–R3ch*); 28. Q–R3, K–K1; 29. B–B5, etc.

(b) 25 . . . K–K1; 26. Q × P, Kt–B1 (26 . . . *R–B1*, 27. *QR–K1*); 27. Q–B7ch, K–Q2; 28. B–B5ch or 28. B–R3, R–K1; 29. R × Kt, P × R; 30. P–Kt7, etc.

26. **Q × Pch**	**K–R1**
27. **Q–R3ch**	**K–Kt1**
28. **B–B5**	**Kt–B1**

The threat was, of course, 29. B–K6ch and mate. 28 . . . B–Kt5 would lose to (e.g.) 29. P–Q5.

29. **B–K6ch**	**Kt × B**
30. **Q × Ktch**	**K–R1**
31. **Q–R3ch**	**K–Kt1**
32. **R × Kt**	

The final sacrifice. Black's reply is forced.

32. . . .	**B × R**
33. **Q–R7ch**	**K–B1**
34. **R–K1**	

And this is the finishing touch. To forestall mate

Black must play 35 . . . B–K4 or 35 . . . Q–K4, either
of which is equivalent to resigning the game.

34.	. . .	B–K4
35.	Q–R8ch	K–K2
36.	Q×Pch!	K–Q3
37.	Q×Bch	K–Q2
38.	Q–KB5ch	K–B3

On 38 . . . K–B2 would follow 39. R–K7ch. Black
must soon be checkmated, anyhow; and Chekover
gallantly gives his adversary this pleasure, otherwise he
would surely have resigned long before.

39. P–Q5ch, K–B4; 40. B–R3ch, K×P; 41.
Q–K4ch, K–B6; 42. B–Kt4ch, K–Kt7; 43. Q–Kt1
mate.

Though Botvinnik is primarily a position player, and
though his construction of the game differs vastly from
Alekhine's, his play reveals, in his discernment of
attacking chances, the greatest possible resemblance
to the brilliant style of the world champion.

CHAPTER VI

SAMUEL RESHEVSKY

Samuel Reshevsky (originally "Rzeszewski") was born on 26th November, 1911, at Ozorkov in Russian Poland. He learned chess before the alphabet, and quickly displayed great talent for it. As a little boy of eight he played such a strong game that he was allowed to perform as an infant prodigy. Together with a member of his family, who played the part of business manager, he made big tours through Central and Western Europe, creating an immense sensation wherever he went. In 1919 he gave some simultaneous displays in Holland, in one of which Euwe, then a youth of eighteen, was the only one of eight participants who managed to draw with him. The same year, at Vienna, he played a serious game against Professor Vidmar, a master of international reputation. The onlookers hardly treated the occasion seriously to begin with, but as Vidmar gradually began to get the worse of it, their attitude changed. In the end the infant prodigy blundered and lost—but it was an honourable defeat.

An invitation to America brought his peregrinations to an end; little Sammy began to settle down, assimilated a normal upbringing and education, and grew up into a normal American citizen. Automatically the name "infant prodigy" was forgotten, and when, years afterwards, he participated in an American tournament, all sensationalism was relegated to the background. Nor were his results of a kind to arouse more than moderate interest. In Pasadena (1932), for instance, he finished behind Alekhine and Kashdan, sharing third place with Dake and Steiner.

His first great success came in the tournament at Syracuse (New York, 1934), which included the best American players, with one or two foreign masters. Reshevsky topped the list with 12 points, followed by Kashdan at 10½, with Dake, Fine, and Kupchik down the list. With his visit to Margate for the Easter congress of 1935 his career as an international grand master began. His one serious competitor, Capablanca, he managed to defeat in a beautiful game which we give later, and his first place in the final list was well earned with 7½ points from nine games.

In the spring of 1936, Reshevsky acquired the title of champion of the United States of America, after a terrible start in which he lost two of his first three games (one newspaper published the score of one of these games, with the caption "The game which lost Reshevsky his chance of the U.S. championship"). This success aroused keen interest in his doings in the grand master tournament at Nottingham in August of the same year. Reshevsky did not disappoint; he shared third to fifth places with Fine and Euwe behind Capablanca and Botvinnik, but in front of Alekhine, Flohr, Lasker, and others. It is curious that the characteristic way in which he forges ahead in individual games is so often mirrored in the progress of his score. Here again an inauspicious start (5 out of 9) was followed by a powerful finish (4½ out of 5)—a triumph of tenacity. He has been accepted as a member of the select group of candidates for world's championship honours ever since.

SAMUEL RESHEVSKY

U.S. champion, in a characteristic pose

(G.226)

Reshevsky devoted the second half of 1937 exclusively to chess. In July he played in the tournament at Kemeri, Latvia, sharing first place with Flohr and Petrov above Alekhine, Keres, Fine, and others. For a long time it looked as if he would win first prize unchallenged, but a setback in the last round (he lost to the Finn, Böök) spoilt his chance.

At first board in the International Team Tournament at Stockholm that August, he led his team to victory.

September 1937 brought new battles. In the exceptionally strong double-round tournament at Semmering-Baden he shared third and fourth places with Capablanca, behind Keres and Fine but in front of Flohr.

After attending the return match Alekhine *v.* Euwe in a journalistic capacity, he participated in the traditional Hastings Christmas tournament, which brought him a resounding victory over Keres, Flohr, Fine, and Mikenas.

Then he returned to America, to confirm his supremacy in U.S. chess with a half-point margin over Fine in the championship tournament, making no mistake in the critical last round.

In the A.V.R.O. tournament he repeated his Nottingham and U.S.A. exploits all over again. A draw from a lost position, then a defeat, a second defeat, a third defeat, then a draw—this was the melancholy tale of his progress in the first five rounds. He seemed condemned to last place. Could anybody recover from such a shocking start—in such company? Reshevsky could—and did. Continually in time-trouble, battling on stubbornly into lengthy end-games, he overhauled Flohr and Capablanca and finally drew abreast of Alekhine and Euwe for an honourable fourth place.

About this time he was very ambitious of a world championship match with Alekhine; dissatisfied with his A.V.R.O. result, he went on to Russia, where, as we have seen, he finished a good second in a strong gathering.

Of late he has been concentrating rather more on his work as an accountant, but a match with Fine for the U.S. Championship is being discussed.

RESHEVSKY AT WORK

First Illustration

Here is the game in which Reshevsky laid the foundation-stone for his speedily attained renown as grand master, on the occasion of his very first appearance in an international master tournament outside America.

S. Reshevsky	J. R. Capablanca
White	*Black*

(From the Margate Easter Congress, 1935.)

QUEEN'S GAMBIT

1.	P–Q4	Kt–KB3
2.	P–QB4	P–K3
3.	Kt–QB3	P–Q4
4.	B–Kt5	QKt–Q2
5.	P×P	

Reshevsky, like Flohr, is partial to this variation, so as firstly to avoid difficult opening problems and

secondly to be able to count on a quiet but lasting
initiative.

5.	. . .	P×P
6.	P–K3	B–K2
7.	B–Q3	O–O
8.	Q–B2	P–B4

8 . . . P–B3 is sounder. Black hopes to profit by the
circumstance that White exchanged on his Q4 without
waiting for . . . P–QB3.

9.	Kt–B3	P–B5

More or less forced; otherwise White will soon play
P×P and eventually concentrate his forces on the
isolated black QP. To make the capture on the ninth
move would have been unwise, as it would concede
Black too great an advantage in development.

10.	B–B5	R–K1
11.	O–O	P–KKt3

An important preamble to his next move. 11 . . .
Kt–B1? would be a blunder because of 12. B×B,
R×B; 13. B×Kt, B×B; 14. Q–B5!, winning the
black QP.

12.	B–R3	Kt–B1

12 . . . P–QR3, followed as soon as possible by . . .
P–QKt4, would have been stronger.

13.	B×B	R×B
14.	B×Kt	B×B
15.	P–QKt3!	

A strong continuation which puts White on top.
15 . . . P×P? 16. Q×QKtP would now cost a Pawn.

Consequently Black must resign himself to the exchange on his QB5, which may have most unpleasant consequences. How is he to recapture? . . . R × P would leave his QP weak, whilst after . . . P × P White's preponderance in the centre would count for far more than Black's majority on the Queen's wing.

15. . . .   **Q–R4**

Holding up 16. P × P, which would allow Black to reply 16 . . . R × P and make deadly use of the pin on the Knight. As the sequel shows, the text move is not wholly satisfactory.

16. **P–QKt4!**

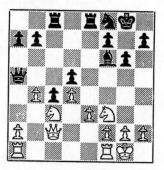

A fine tactical *coup* which serves to produce a pseudo-isolation of Black's QBP and QP and eventually trouble Black with persistent threats to his QP.

16. . . .   **Q–Q1**

The only move. After 16 . . . Q × KtP; 17. QR–Kt1 (stronger than 17. *Kt × P, Q–Q3*), Q–Q3; 18. R × P with the three threats 19. R × QRP, 19. R–Kt5 and

19. KR–Kt1, Black's position would speedily become untenable.

> 17. **Q–R4**

With threats of 18. Q×P and 18. Q–Kt5 which force Black's reply.

> 17. . . .   **P–QR3**
> 18. **P–Kt5**!

The strategical point of 16. P–QKt4. White gains possession of the square QKt5 and this makes the isolation of the Black QBP and QP an accomplished fact.

> 18. . . .   **R–K3**

The threat was 19. P×P, R–R1; 20. Q–Kt5. Exchanging on his QKt4 would cost Black a Pawn likewise.

> 19. **QR–Kt1**!

Threatening 20. P×P, R×P (20 . . . *P×P*, 21. *R–Kt7*); 21. Q–Kt5 winning a Pawn. 19. P×P at once would not be so good, on account of 19 . . . R×P; 20. Q–Kt5, R–R4!, White being unable now to capture the QKtP because of 21 . . . R–Kt1, 22. Q–B6, R–Kt3; and the Queen is trapped.

Apart from this, the text move robs Black of all possibility of blocking the Queen's side by . . . P–QR4 followed by . . . P–Kt3. Let us try: 19 . . . P–QR4; 20. P–Kt6!, R×P; 21. R×R (the object is to win the QP without giving up the blockade of the QBP; consequently not 21. *Kt×P, R×R*, 22. *Kt×Bch*,

$Q \times Kt$, etc.), 21 . . . $Q \times R$; 22. R–Kt1 and White
picks up the black Queen's side Pawns one by one.

| 19. . . . | **R–Kt1** |
| 20. **R–Kt2** | |

Threatening 21. KR–Kt1 followed by 22. $P \times P$
($R \times P$; 23. $Q \times R$).

| 20. . . . | **B–K2** |

Black is still aiming at 21 . . . P–QR4 and is now
ready to reply to 22. P–Kt6 with B–Kt5 (gaining time
by attacking the undefended Knight) followed by
23 . . . Kt–Q2 or 23 . . . $R \times KtP$, e.g. 23. R–B1,
$B \times Kt$; 24. $R \times B$, $R \times P$. If White postpones 22.
P–Kt6, then Black plays a Pawn on to that square
himself, bringing his opponent's attack to a full stop.

| 21. **P $\times$ P** | |

Naturally White does not allow the Queen's side to
be blocked.

21. . . .	**R $\times$ RP**
22. **Q–B2**	**Kt–K3**
23. **KR–Kt1**	**R–R2**
24. **P–QR4**	

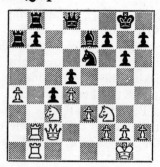

Concluding, for the moment, the operations he inaugurated with 16. P–QKt4. The black Pawn complex (QP and QBP) is demonstrably isolated; Black must put up with protracted pressure along the open QKt file. Reshevsky has gained a clear positional advantage through splendid tactics. Now the game enters on a new phase: White gradually strengthens his position.

24. ...	**Kt–B2**
25. **Kt–K5**	

Threatening to win the exchange by 26. Kt–B6.

25. ...	**Q–K1**
26. **P–B4**	

Reshevsky foresees well that Black will not be able to make anything out of the backward KP which this produces. The threat of P–B5, starting a strong attack on the King's side, is now in the air. First, however, come a few moves which do not alter the situation to any considerable extent. (One might surmise that Reshevsky would normally be in time-trouble about here!)

26 ... **P–B3**; 27. **Kt–Kt4, Q–Q2**; 28. **P–R3, K–Kt2**; 29. **Kt–B2, B–R6**; 30. **R–R2, B–Q3**; 31. **Kt(B2)–Q1, P–B4**.

So as not to have continually to reckon with the possibility of P–B5 or P–K4.

32. **Kt–Kt5!**	**R–R4**
33. **Kt×Kt**	**B×Kt**
34. **Kt–B3!**	

The manoeuvre with the white Knight was very

fine, exchanging off the hostile Knight without yielding up the blockade of the black QBP. Note that the
blockading Knight simultaneously attacks the QP.
The disappearance of the black Knight opens up the
square QKt5 for the use of the white Rooks.

34.	. . .	Q–K3
35.	Q–B2	P–Kt3
36.	Q–B3	R–Q1
37.	R(R2)–Kt2	

Though it seems now that Black can no longer prevent the fall of his Queen's Pawn, Capablanca defends
as well as possible and finds a pretty resource against
the threat of R–Kt5.

37.	. . .	Q–K2!

So as to reply to 38. R–Kt5 with 38 . . . R×R;
39. R×R, Q–R6, after which the passed Pawn would
suddenly become strong, e.g. 40. Kt×P, P–B6; 41.
Kt×B, P–B7; 42. Kt–K6ch, K–R1, and the Pawn
will queen.

38.	R–Kt4	R–Q2
39.	K–R1	B–Q1
40.	P–Kt4	

The Queen's Pawn cannot be won directly, so White
goes to improve his position by a demonstration on the
King's side. This move threatens 41. P×P, which after
the reply 41 . . . P×P would saddle Black with yet
another weak Pawn, at his KB4; apart from this, the
open KKt file would spell danger for the black King.

40.	. . .	P×P

The best.

41.	**P×P**	**Q–Q3**

41. . . . Q–R5ch would be merely waste of time:
42. K–Kt2.

42.	**K–Kt1**	**B–B2**
43.	**K–B2**	

The white King is heading for QB2, where it supports the Knight. This would rob Black's . . . Q–R6 of its sting, so that White could safely go to win the QP by R–Kt5.

43. . . .	**R–B2 !**

Capablanca finds a defence once again. He threatens to counter-attack dangerously, commencing with 44 . . . P–KKt4, e.g. 44. K–K2, P–KKt4; 45. P–B5, R–B3, and White has no adequate parry against the threat of 46 . . . R–KR3, since 46. R–KR1 would leave the Rook on Kt4 unprotected. Hence White's next is practically forced, though it frees the important square KB4 for the black Queen.

44.	**P–Kt5**	**B–Q1**
45.	**K–K2**	**B×P**

Here Black misses the best continuation and soon gets into a hopeless situation. 45 . . . Q–K3 would have given White much more trouble, threatening 46 . . . Q–B4, with an invasion to B7 or Q6 in the air.

46.	**R×KtP**	**Q–R6**
47.	**K–Q2 !**	

See the note to 43. K–B2. Everything is adequately protected on the Queen's side; the black Queen can do nothing from QR6, and White returns immediately to the attack, which, thanks to his possession of the open QKt file, speedily clinches the issue.

47. · · ·		**B–K2**
48. **R–Kt7**		**R × RP**

One last despairing attempt. Passive play would be useless, e.g. 48 . . . Q–Q3; 49. R(Kt7)–Kt5, R×R; 50. P×R!, R–B4; 51. P–Kt6 and wins.

49. **Q×P**

To capture the Rook would be a bad blunder: 49. Kt×R?? Q–Q6ch; 50. K–B1 (50. *K–K1, B–R5ch*), B–R6ch; 51. R(Kt7)–Kt2, P–B6 and wins. With the text move, on the other hand, White wins the QBP as well, since there is nothing to be done against the threat of 50. Q–Kt5.

49. · · ·		**R–R4**
50. **Q×P**		

The race is run. Reshevsky's strategy has been crowned with complete success. He has won both the Pawns he isolated.

The white King is, rather remarkably, safer in the centre of the board than the black in his castled domain. Incidentally, an illustration of the significance of a strong centre.

50.	. . .	**R–R4**
51.	**K–Q3**	**Q–R1**
52.	**Q–K6**	**Q–R6**

Costs a piece and precipitates the end.

53. **R–Q7**

There is now no parrying the simultaneous threats of 54. R(Kt1)–Kt7 and 54. R–Kt3.

53. . . .   **R(R4)–KB4**

Countering the first threat (if 54. R(Kt1)–Kt7, the Bishop simply moves away), but not the second.

54.	**R–Kt3**	**Q–R8**
55.	**R × B**	**Q–KB8ch**
56.	**K–Q2**	Resigns

This game gives us a very good picture of Reshevsky's style. Quiet construction of the game (5. P × P) masks enterprising plans (the intention to castle on the Queen's side), and if provoked (8 . . . P–B4), he is quite willing to "mix it," and knows how to seize his chances in supreme fashion (15. P–QKt3!, 16. P–QKt4!, and 18. P–Kt5!). In the middle-game he is daring, and often enough decides on seemingly risky manœuvres which not even Flohr and Botvinnik would voluntarily undertake. (40. P–Kt4 followed by the march of the King.) Fortified by strong nerves, devout optimism, great self-confidence, a philosophical temperament and a tremendous weight of experience, he feels confident in any position that is even remotely presentable, and up to any task the world of his opponents may present him.

Second Illustration

As second game we print one of somewhat the same genre but with Reshevsky as Black.

I. KASHDAN   S. RESHEVSKY
White   *Black*

(Played in the U.S. Championship, 1938)

QUEEN'S GAMBIT ACCEPTED, NOTTINGHAM VARIATION

1. Kt–KB3	P–Q4
2. P–Q4	Kt–KB3
3. P–B4	P–K3
4. P–KKt3	P×P
5. Q–R4ch	

This move, in connexion with the fianchetto of the King's Bishop, is the hall-mark of the Nottingham variation. The first six or seven moves can be transposed in various ways.

5. . . .	QKt–Q2
6. B–Kt2	P–QR3
7. Q×BP	P–B4

Black could also play 7 . . . P–QKt4 at once, for
8. Q–B6 merely wastes time: 8 . . . R–R2!; 9. B–B4,
B–Kt2! (Capablanca–Reshevsky, Nottingham, 1936.)
10. Q×BP would fail through 10 . . . Q×Q·
11. B×Q, B×Kt.

        8. **O–O**   **P–QKt4**
        9. **Q–Q3**

9. Q–B2 was preferable. Through the manœuvre
Q–R4ch and Q×BP in this variation, the white
Queen comes to be somewhat exposed, hence it is
advisable to retire her to a safe square as soon as
possible.

        9. . . .   **B–Kt2**
      10. **P–QR4**

The well-known way of smashing up the formation
⸗f Pawns on R3, Kt4, B4; but here it fails to obtain
the result desired. White could have secured a drawish
position by 10. P×P.

      10. . . .   **P–Kt5**
      11. **QKt–Q2**

Apparently coming into fine play via QKt3 or QB4.

      11. . . .   **P×P!**

Far from a mere simple exchange, but a pretty
combination by which Black gains important time. The
point is that the natural reply 12. Kt×P would lose:
12 . . . Kt–K4! 13. Q–K3 (forced), 13 . . . Kt(B3)–
Kt5; 14. Q–B4, P–Kt4!, and the white Queen has no
move. Consequently White must recapture on Q4

with the Queen, which enables Black to gain time in developing his King's Bishop.

12.	Q×QP	B–B4
13.	Q–R4	

The white Queen leads a fugitive existence. 13. Q–Q3 would have been just as unsatisfactory.

13.	. . .	O–O
14.	P–Kt3	

Weakening his QB3. 14. Kt–K1 would have offered better prospects for the respectable development of his pieces.

14.	. . .	Kt–Q4!

Very good. After the practically forced exchange of Queens, Black's pieces work well together.

15.	Q×Q	KR×Q

Black is ahead in development and can also make capital out of the weakness of White's QB3. These factors are not decisive in themselves, especially as Kashdan defends very well; but Reshevsky manages not only to maintain his advantage but gradually to increase it.

16.	B–Kt2	Kt–B6
17.	KR–K1	QR–B1
18.	QR–B1	Kt–B3

The Knight on B6 is indirectly protected, 19. B×Kt? P×B; 20. R×P?, B×Pch losing the exchange.

19.	P–K3

Now White threatens 20. B × Kt in earnest.

19. . . .	**B–R2**
20. **Kt–B4**	

White seems to have evaded his difficulties already, since Black cannot consolidate the situation of his advanced Knight any further. If 20 . . . Kt(B3)–K5, then 21. Kt–Kt5 would be a very strong reply; whilst 20 . . . Kt(B3)–Q4 can hardly be correct, since Black would then have continually to reckon with the possibility of . . . P–K4.

20. . . .	**Kt(B6)–K5**
21. **Kt–Kt5**	**B–Q4**
22. **Kt × Kt**	**Kt × Kt**
23. **R(K1)–Q1**	**P–B3**

Black must be on the alert against premature simplification, e.g. 23 . . . B × Kt; 24. R × Rch, R × R; 25. R × B, R–Q8ch; 26. B–B1, R × Bch; 27. K × R, Kt–Q7ch; 28. K–K2, Kt × R; 29. P × Kt and White has a beautiful game; he threatens to isolate Black's QKtP by 30. P–R5 and then win it, whilst Black cannot play 29 . . . P–QR4 himself because of 30. B–K5 (threatening 31. B–B7), 30 . . . B–Kt3; 31. B–Q6 and White wins by advancing his passed Pawn.

24. **K–B1**	**K–B1**

24 . . . B × Ktch would still achieve nothing: 25. P × B, Kt–B4; 26. B–Q4 followed by 27. B × Kt and the game would be drawn, through the Bishops being on squares of opposite colour.

25. **B–Q4**

With every move White is gaining command of more of the board, but Reshevsky now takes care to put an end to the process.

25.	. . .	**B × B**
26.	**R × B**	

Not 26 . . . P × B, which would lose at least a Pawn by 26 . . . Kt–B6.

26.	. . .	**Kt–Q7ch !**

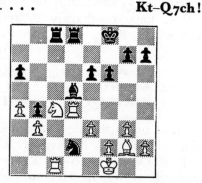

A painful surprise for White, who apparently had reckoned only with 26 . . . B × Ktch, which would yield Black the advantage by 27. P × B, R × R; 28. P × R, Kt–Q7ch; 29. K–K2, Kt–Kt6!; 30. R–Kt1, Kt × Pch; 31. K–Q3, R–Q1! But White has better: 27. R(B1) × B, and this move even gives him the upper hand, as 27 . . . Kt–Q7ch fails against 28. R × Kt, whilst both 27 . . . R(B1) × R and 27 . . . R(Q1) × R lose.

The text move produces a far-reaching simplification which gives Black's advantage concrete form.

27. **R × Kt**

Forced.

27. . . .	**B × Bch!**
28. **K–K1**	

Not 28. K × B?, R × R and wins.

28. . . .	**R × R**
29. **K × R**	**B–Q4**

Threatening 30 . . . B × Kt, after which the protected passed Pawn would be extremely dangerous,
e.g. 31. P × B (31. *R × B?, R × R*; 32. *P × R, P–QR4,*
and wins easily), 31 . . . R–B4 followed by 32. P–QR4.

30. **K–Q3**	**P–K4**
31. **P–K4**	**B–K3**
32. **R–B2**	**K–K2**
33. **Kt–Q2**	

Naturally White must get rid of the pin on the file
as soon as possible.

33. . . .	**R × R**
34. **K × R**	**K–Q3**
35. **K–Q3**	**K–B4**

Now see what the simplification started by 26 . . . Kt–Q 7 has produced. White's position exhibits two serious weaknesses, one material (on QKt3) and one positional (on Q4). White's Knight cannot move, owing to the threat on the QKtP; his King must keep an eye on the square Q4, lest the black King invade it. Consequently the white pieces are almost completely immobilized. The Bishop is vastly superior to the Knight; for instance, it can move at will along the diagonal (Black's) KKt1 to K3 without giving up the pressure on White's QKtP, and this circumstance confronts White with the danger of becoming movebound.

In the ensuing technical phase of the game Reshevsky contrives to resolve his advantage into an efficient win.

36.	**K–K3**	**P–Kt3**
37.	**K–Q3**	**P–B4**
38.	**P–B3**	

The only chance of putting up serious resistance lay in 38. P×P, e.g. 38 . . . P×P; 39. P–B3, B–Q4; 40. K–K3, P–B5ch; 41. P×P, P×Pch; 42. K–Q3!, P–QR4; 43. Kt–K4ch, K–B3; 44. Kt–Q2, etc.

The text move allows the black King access to K3 without gaining K4 for the Knight.

38.	**. . .**	**P–B5!**
39.	**P×P**	**P×P**

Black has acquired two more advantages, the majority of Pawns on the King's side and the certainty of his King's being able to penetrate to Q5—this latter through his being able to exhaust White of moves.

40.	**P–R4**	**P–R3**
41.	**P–QR5**	

In vain White struggles against the surrender of his Q4.

41.	. . .	**B–Q2 !**

Threatening the unmeetable 42 . . . B–Kt4ch; 43. K–B2, K–Q5.

42.	**K–B2**

If 42. Kt–B4, then 42 . . . B–Kt4 would be even worse.

42.	. . .	**K–Q5**

The rest is easy.

43. **Kt–B4, B–K3**; 44. **Kt–Q2, K–K6**; 45. **K–Q1, K–B7**; 46. **K–B2, K–K7**; 47. **K–B1, P–R4!**

Threatening 48 . . . P–Kt4; 49. P×P, P–R5, etc. There is now no preventing the promotion of Black's KRP.

48. **P–K5, P–Kt4**; 49. **Kt–K4, P×P**; 50. **Kt–Kt5, P–R6!** 51. **Kt×B, P–R7**; 52. **Kt×Pch, K×P.**

White resigns.

An outstanding positional game, characterized by the various tactical niceties through which Reshevsky strengthened his hold on the game and by the cleverness with which he managed to retain his advantage, in a variety of forms, through all sorts of simplifications.

Third Illustration

Reshevsky often wins with Black. He prefers defences which encourage his opponent to attack; there arise lively positions in which his tactical preparedness counts for a lot. The next two games illustrate this well.

DR. E. LASKER   S. RESHEVSKY
White   *Black*

(Played in the tournament at Nottingham, 1936.)

QUEEN'S GAMBIT ACCEPTED

1. **P–Q4, P–Q4;** 2. **P–QB4, P×P;** 3. **Kt–KB3, Kt–KB3;** 4. **P–K3, P–K3;** 5. **B×P, P–B4;** 6. **Kt–B3.**

Of late, 6. O–O followed by 7. Q–K2 has been almost exclusively played. It is not certain which is the better system.

6. . . .   **P–QR3**
7. **O–O**

The "classical" continuation 7. P–QR4 has gone completely out of favour.

7. . . .   **P–QKt4**
8. **B–Q3**

Once he has played 6. Kt–QB3, it is preferable to retire this Bishop to Kt3. White must go for the breakthrough by P–Q5 in this variation.

8. . . .   **P×P**

This exchange is important, to fix the centre formation. White's KP disappears, and his QP can neither capture nor march forward.

9.	P×P	B–Kt2
10.	B–Kt5	B–K2
11.	Q–K2	O–O
12.	QR–Q1	

White is aiming at building up a strong attacking position by Kt–K5 and P–B4, but Reshevsky manages to thwart this plan by a few simple moves.

12.	. . .	QKt–Q2
13.	Kt–K5	Kt–Q4!

Very troublesome for White. After 14. B×B, Q×B (14 . . . *Kt×Kt??*; 15. *B×RPch!*) 15. P–B4 (or 15. *Kt×Kt, B×Kt*), 15 . . . Kt×Kt(B6); 16. P×Kt, KR–B1 Black has the better Pawn formation, whilst White's attacking chances are somewhat problematical.

14. **B–B1**

To avoid exchanges, a good plan for the attacker as a rule; but the move loses time and allows Black to saddle White with a backward Pawn on his QB3.

14.	. . .	Kt×Kt(B6)
15.	P×Kt	Kt–B3
16.	P–QR4	

A pretty Pawn sacrifice which White had apparently had in mind when making his preceding move. After

16 . . . P×P; 17. P–QB4 or 17. B–Kt2 followed by 18. P–QB4, White really would get good attacking chances, his command of the important central square Q5 insuring him against all possibility of counter-attack.

There is one serious drawback—that Black need not accept the sacrifice.

16. . . .   Q–Q4!

17. P–KB4 would, as things stand, only mean creating new weaknesses, so White's Knight has to go back again.

17. Kt–B3   KR–B1!

Black has now an excellent game. The best for White is now 18. P×P, P×P; 19. B×P, R×P; 20. Q–K5, but he would still have inadequate compensation for the isolation of his Queen's Pawn.

18. B–Kt2   Kt–K5!

Very strongly played, again. Equally after 19. B×Kt, Q×B; 20. Q×Q, B×Q, and after 19. P×P, P×P; 20. B×P, Kt×QBP; 21. B×Kt, R×B, Black would have an overwhelming position. Yet White should have chosen one of these continuations.

19. R–B1   Kt–Kt4!

Black employs simple methods, yet clarifies his advantage with every move. Lasker does not get a single opportunity to exploit his redoubtable ability in involved positions.

20. **P × P**   **P × P**

Not 20 . . . Kt × Ktch; 21. Q × Kt and White would suddenly have good counter-chances.

21. **B × KtP**

Losing outright. 21. Kt–K1 was necessary, although White's position would hardly have been tenable after 21 . . . Kt–R6ch; 22. K–R1, Kt–B5, followed by . . . Kt × B.

21. . . .   **Kt × Ktch**

22. **P × Kt**

As a consequence of his preceding move, White cannot recapture with the Queen (22. Q × Kt, Q × B), and this proves fatal.

22. . . .   **Q–Kt4ch**

23. **K–R1**   **Q–Kt5!**

With the threat of 24 . . . B × Pch, against which nothing can be done. White resigns.

Fourth Illustration

S. Landau	S. Reshevsky
White	*Black*

(Played in the Kemeri, Latvia, tournament, 1937.)

QUEEN'S GAMBIT ACCEPTED

1. **P–Q4, P–Q4;** 2. **P–QB4, P×P;** 3. **Kt–KB3, Kt–KB3;** 4. **P–K3, P–QR3;** 5. **B×P, P–K3;** 6. **O–O, P–B4;** 7. **Q–K2, P–QKt4;** 8. **B–Q3.**

Concerning the opening, see the last game.

White has omitted Kt–QB3 here. He now wants to attack Black's Queen's wing by P–QR4; in this connexion, his KB is better placed on Q3 than Kt3.

8. . . .	P×P

Selecting the same construction as in the preceding game, but in the changed circumstances it does not yield him a wholly satisfactory game.

9. **P×P**	**B–Kt2**
10. **P–QR4 !**	**P–Kt5**
11. **QKt–Q2**	**B–K2**
12. **Kt–B4**	**P–QR4**

Black could not permit 13. P–R5.

13. **B–B4**	**O–O**
14. **KR–Q1**	**Kt–B3**
15. **B–K5**	**Kt–Q4**

With the same idea as in the last game: Black wants

to ease his task by exchanges, but this time he meets
with more difficulty.

16.	Q–K4	P–Kt3
17.	Q–Kt4	Kt–B3
18.	Q–B4	Kt–R4

Reshevsky manœuvres quite cleverly, keeping his
opponent occupied all the time so that he cannot
easily develop his attack. The situation, however,
remains difficult for Black.

19. **Q–K3**

Sagely played. After 19. Q–R6, Kt×B; 20. P×Kt,
B×Kt; 21. B×P (21. *P×B, B–Kt4* and wins), 21 . . .
BP×B; 22. R×Q, QR×R; 23. P×B, Kt–B5 (threat-
ening 24 . . . B–Kt4! 25. Q×B, Kt–R6ch or 24 . . .
R–B4 and . . . R–R4) White, in spite of his extra
material, would be in a very awkward corner, as his
Queen is in peril of her life.

19.	. . .	R–B1
20.	QR–B1	Kt×B

This and the two following moves are very deep.
Reshevsky, although still in difficulties, sets his
opponent a diabolic trap.

21.	P×Kt	B–B4
22.	Q–R6	Q–K2
23.	Kt–Kt5?	

This is just the move Black was hoping for. 23.
Kt×P? would also have been bad, because of 23 . . .
B×Kt; 24. P×B, Q–R2 attacking the Knight and

the KBP simultaneously; but 23. B–K2 would have left White excellently placed.

The text move loses.

23. . . .   **P–B3**
24. **P×P**

It goes without saying that White would have rejected 23. Kt–Kt5 if he had realized what was coming now, for it is already too late to save the situation; 24. Kt–K4 or 24. Kt–R3 would be answered by 24 . . . P×P, while 24 B×P would give a piece away, not for an attack but for nothing.

24. . . .   **B×Pch**

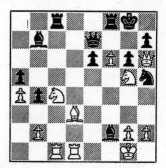

A thunderbolt out of a clear sky. Lulled by roseate dreams a moment ago, White is rudely awakened by elemental violence.

25. **K×B**

25. K–R1 would have been just as useless, for instance 25 . . . R×P; 26. Kt×QRP (otherwise White remains a Pawn behind in a bad position), 26 . .

R×R; 27. R×R, B–K6; 28. R–K1, B×Kt; 29. Q×B, R–B8ch winning the Queen. After the text move White has no more choice at all.

25. . . .	Q×Pch
26. Kt–B3	

A King move would allow mate in one move or two.

26. . . .	B×Kt
27. P×B	Q×BPch
28. K–Kt1	R–B5!

The threat of 29 . . . R–Kt5ch is crushing.

29. Q×R

Brings only momentary relief.

29. . . .	Kt×Q

Threatening mate in two distinct ways.

30. B–B1	R–B4

The same little idea as before, but now White has no Queen to throw herself gallantly on to the flames.

31. R–Q8ch	K–Kt2
32. R–Q7ch	K–R3

White resigns.

We see that the American champion can institute splendid combinations. His talent is, as we have observed, truly many-sided.

CHAPTER VII

REUBEN FINE

R. Fine was born in New York on 11th October, 1914, and became acquainted with chess at an early age without taking it very seriously. In his fifteenth year he suddenly began to progress, and speedily developed into a strong player. In 1932 he took part in the tournament at Pasadena (see the chapter on Reshevsky), but without success; he shared last place with J. Bernstein, Factor, and Reinfeld. A year later, however, he had acquired such a reputation through local successes that he was elected a member of the U.S. team for the Folkestone Team Tournament. This was his first appearance on the European stage, and he assisted his country to victory in promising style. In the tournament at Syracuse (New York, 1934) he shared third and fourth places with Dake behind Reshevsky and Kashdan, and a year later (July, 1935) he scored a brilliant success at the American Chess Federation's thirty-sixth congress at Milwaukee, winning the top tournament with eight points out of ten games, above Dake (second) and Kashdan (third)—a remarkable feat, since Kashdan was then considered the strongest player in America. Reshevsky did not participate in this tournament.

On the strength of this achievement he was selected to play at the U.S.A.'s top board in the International Team Tournament at Warsaw (August 1935). He started rather badly (it is said he had a thoroughly seasick crossing), but pulled up towards the end and

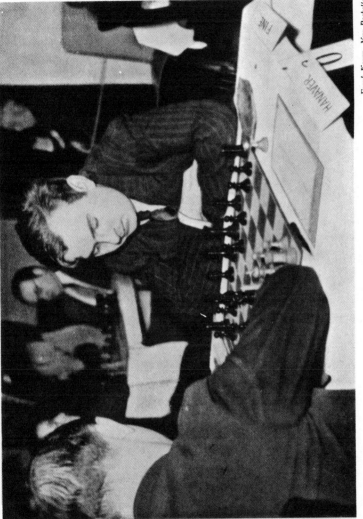

Photo   *Frank Kenny, New Rochelle*

REUBEN FINE

Playing in his second U.S. Championship

(G.226)

played a worthy part in his team's victory. As a sequel
to the "Olympiad," a tournament of ten was organized
at Lodz, and there Fine came second, together with
Kolski, behind Tartakover. This was his first individual tournament in Europe. A few months later
he scored a sensational success in the Christmas congress at Hastings, beating Flohr and taking first prize.
Now he suddenly began to be considered a candidate
for the world's championship—as Alekhine, incidentally, had predicted he would many years before.

1936 began with a little disappointment. Marshall,
still titular champion of the U.S.A. as there had been
no championship tournaments for a long time, relinquished his title voluntarily, and thus the American
Chess Federation found themselves with the task of
organizing a tournament for the title. A series of
qualifying tournaments produced a final tourney of
sixteen. Fine started favourite but could finish no
higher than third, equal with Treysman. Reshevsky
was the new champion, with Simonson second and
Kashdan fifth. It was about here that Reshevsky was
suddenly revealed as Fine's "bogey-man"; another
three years were to elapse before Fine could score his
first win against him.

In 1936 he returned to stay more than a year and a
half in Europe, during which time he played in one
tournament after another, registering a series of fine
successes. Towards the end his results—evidently
through staleness—began to deteriorate. The first
tournament in this period was at Amsterdam, where he
took first place with 8½ points out of 11 (Euwe 7½,
Keres and Dr. Tartakover each 6½, Bogolyubov and

Maroczy each 6). The Nottingham (1936) tournament followed which we have already mentioned more than once (see, for instance, under Reshevsky).

Fine settled awhile in Amsterdam. In October he competed in a tournament of eight organized by a socialist newspaper company and finished first, together with Euwe, Alekhine being half a point behind in third place. In the Hastings Christmas tournament he came second to Alekhine, who beat him in their individual encounter after Fine had rushed away with a sequence of seven straight wins. Fine made a bee-line from Hastings direct to Sweden, where he took part in several tournaments, the most outstanding result of this trip being his beating Stahlberg in a match by 5-3.

Then came a trip to Russia, where he won two small events in which Botvinnik did not compete. The Margate Easter tournament enabled him to revenge himself over Alekhine for the defeat at Hastings. He and Keres both beat the world champion in their individual encounters, and finished together in first place. This tournament represented the culmination, for the time being, of his success; months of play without a moment's respite had begun to sap his powers, and in the tournament at Ostend which immediately followed Margate he received a serious warning. In the middle of this tournament he rushed over to London to give a simultaneous display, returning to complete his schedule of games at high pressure. In the circumstances he did well to share the final first place with Grob and Keres; but in doing so he lost no fewer than three games, a result the more

perturbing as the chess world had become accustomed
to seeing him lose only on the rarest occasions. A two-
months' rest ensued, apparently not long enough, for
his performance in the strong tournament at Kemeri
in June 1937 was a débâcle; he finished ninth out
of eighteen, and—what was even more painful—could
only amass a single point against the seven leaders,
Flohr, Petrov, Reshevsky, Alekhine, Keres, A. Steiner,
and Tartakover. Was staleness alone to blame for this
setback? The historian gropes in the dark; he can
only record that a month afterwards Fine announced
his engagement to Miss Keesing. Within another
month he was married and had gone off to take part
in the very strong tournament at Semmering-Baden,
where he really threw himself into the fray. He came
second to Keres in front of Capablanca, Reshevsky,
Flohr, Eliskases, Ragozin, and Petrov. It was here
that he had one of the most annoying experiences of
his career: two Pawns up in a Bishop v. Knight ending
against Reshevsky, he could not win! His score, in an
event of level results, made a curious showing: two
wins, no losses, twelve draws!

From October till December he acted as "second"
to Euwe in the return match for the world's title, and
we need make no secret of the fact that—in spite of his
principal's disappointing result—he discharged this
task nobly. That after these weeks of exertion and
tension he could only tie for fourth and fifth places with
Flohr in the Christmas tournament at Hastings was
hardly surprising.

In January, 1938, he sailed with his wife for New York.
Our young grand master had had enough of chess for

the time being, and returned to complete his mathematical studies; but in the meantime he competed in
the American championship tournament in March,
with the result already reported: Reshevsky 13, Fine
12½, Simonson 11, Horowitz 10, Kashdan 9½, etc. In
their last-round game, though playing White, he could
make no impression on Reshevsky and was glad in
the end to accept a draw.

Then came several months of rest and quiet re-
search on the openings for his revision of *Modern Chess
Openings*, until October, when he returned to Holland
to score the success of his life. In the first six rounds of
the A.V.R.O. tournament he beat Botvinnik, Reshevsky, Euwe, Flohr, and Alekhine and drew with
Capablanca—surely one of the most brilliant bursts in
chess history. And he missed a win against Capablanca!

Then came a landslide, and he could only snatch
three points out of his remaining eight games; but he
had done enough to assure himself of first place.

FINE IN ACTION

First Illustration

The game which follows took a fairly quiet course.
Queens came off early, and there were no combinations
of note. Fine played pretty keenly withal: in the very
beginning he conceded the "minor exchange" and
the Pawn majority on the Queen's wing, convinced
that his superior mobility on other fronts would count
for more. Keen and efficient play is required, in a case

like this, to make the abstract advantage turn the scale against the concrete. Fine succeeds convincingly.

R. FINE   G. MAROCZY
White   *Black*

(Played in the Zandvoort tournament, 1936.)

ORTHODOX QUEEN'S GAMBIT

1. P–Q4, P–K3; 2. P–QB4, Kt–KB3; 3. Kt–QB3, P–Q4; 4. Kt–B3, B–K2; 5. B–Kt5, QKt–Q2; 6. P–K3, O–O; 7. R–B1, P–B3; 8. B–Q3, P–KR3; 9. B–B4.

9. B–R4 is more usual; the text move is "sharper" in so far as it permits Black to exchange off White's QB for a Knight. The resulting situation is difficult to assess, White's command of greater terrain being balanced against Black's retention of his two Bishops.

Fine often makes moves in the opening which sharpen, or rather could sharpen, the conflict. He does not go in for direct attack, but strives after some positional aim in a more or less provocative way. If his opponent takes up the gauntlet, a lively game quickly ensues, in which it usually becomes evident that Fine has seen far more deeply into the position than his opponent.

9. . . .   P × P

Black would better have played 9 . . . Kt–R4 at once if he is going to play it at all, e.g. 10. B–K5, Kt × B; 11. P × Kt, P–KKt3; 12. O–O, B–Q2; 13.

Q–Q2, P×P; 14. B×BP, Q–B2; 15. Kt–K4, QR–Q1; 16. Q–B3, B–B1; 17. P–KKt4, P–KB4!, with good play for Black (Thomas *v.* Lasker, Nottingham, 1936).

10. **B×BP**	**Kt–R4**

Once Black has given up the centre, 10 . . . Kt–Q4 deserves preference. The point is that then, after the attacked Bishop moves, 11 . . . Kt×Kt can be played, White having to recapture with the Pawn, since otherwise he would lose the exchange by . . . B–Kt5. The blocking of the QB file thus produced would ease Black's task considerably, and for this reason White does best, after 10 . . . Kt–Q4, to allow Black to capture his QB by continuing 11. O–O.

11. **B–K5** !	**Kt×B**
12. **P×Kt**	

Threatening to win a piece by 13. P–KKt4. We now perceive the important distinction between the continuations 10 . . . Kt–Q4 and 10 . . . Kt–R4; the first allows Black to play 11 . . . Kt×B and concentrate unhindered on the task of bringing his QB into play, whilst the second, adopted here, leaves his Knight most awkwardly placed, so that he has to postpone the important job of getting out the Bishop until he has attended to its security.

12. **. . .**	**Q×Qch**

Black exchanges Queens to eliminate the danger of a direct attack, at any rate.

13. **R×Q**	**P–KKt3**

Black has the two Bishops and the better Pawn position. His preponderence on the Queen's side is a clear advantage in itself, since one of White's Pawns on the other wing is doubled; whilst the Bishop pair is a certain guarantee for the future. All these factors are not quite enough to counterbalance his difficulties in developing, however, as Fine has foreseen.

14. **P–KKt4**   **Kt–Kt2**

Not a beautiful square for the Knight. The consequences of the inferior 10 . . . Kt–R4 are becoming more and more clearly apparent.

15. **Kt–K4**

Cancelling out one of Black's advantages already; White can now play Kt–B6ch whenever he chooses, as good as forcing the reply . . . B×Kt, so that Black's better Bishop disappears.

15. . . .   **P–R3**
16. **P–KR4**   **P–QKt4**
17. **B–K2**

It is just as well to retire this piece to a square on which it is quite immune from further chivvying by Pawns.

17. . . .   **P–QB4**
18. **O–O**

Very well played. Superficially it might seem good to forego castling, leaving the Rook at R1 and playing for a King's side attack, e.g. with P–R5 in mind (which would induce Black to play . . . P–KKt4 so that White could then break through by P–B4). Fine does the job more simply and safely. He prefers to base his operations on the Queen's file, and his judgment is speedily vindicated.

18. . . .   **B–Kt2**
19. **Kt–B6ch**

Accurately timed. Black must capture, otherwise 20 R–Q7 decides.

19. . . .   **B×Kt**
20. **P×B**   **Kt–K1**
21. **P–Kt5**   **B–Q4**

Black has nothing better in face of the threat of 22. R–Q7.

22. **Kt–K5**

Threatening to win the exchange by 23 Kt–Q7!

22. . . .   **Kt–Q3**
23. **P–B3**!

Threatening to win a piece by 24. P–K4. If 23 . . . KR–Q1; 24. P–K4, B–Kt2 (24 . . . *B×RP?;* 25. *Kt–B6, R–Q2;* 26. *P–K5* and wins); 25. R–Q2, Kt–K1; 26. R(B1)–Q1, R×R; 27. R×R and wins easily through his possession of the Queen's file. Black is at a loss for a satisfactory reply. [We have a feeling 23. Kt–Q7 would have been even stronger: 23 . . . KR–B1; 24. Kt–Kt6.—*Translators.*]

23. . . .   **Kt–B5**

Black has already had to give back the minor exchange, and now he sees his Pawn majority on the Queen's side disappear. The ensuing exchanges leave his Pawns badly scattered, and soon one of them must go.

24. **B×Kt, B×B;** 25. **Kt×B, P×Kt;** 26. **R–B1, QR–Kt1;** 27. **R–KB2, R–Kt5;** 28. **P–R3!**

Driving the Rook to an inferior square.

28 . . . **R–R5;** 29. **R–B3, R–Q1;** 30. **R(B2)–B2.**

Winning the Pawn on B4.

30 . . . **R–Q4.**

30 . . . R–Kt1 or 30 . . . R–Q8ch; 31. K–Kt2, R–QKt8 would be no better. White would not capture the Pawn at once, but would first bring his King to KKt3.

31. **P–B4, P–K4;** 32. **R×P, R×R;** 33. **R×R, KP×P;** 34. **KP×P, P×P;** 35. **RP×P, R–Q7;** 36. **R×P, R×P;** 37. **R–B8ch, K–R2;** 38. **R–B8.**

White's efforts are crowned by his sudden ability to profit by the bad position of his opponent's King.

Black now played 38 . . . R–Kt2, and immediately resigned, realizing the hopelessness of further resistance. White need only keep an eye on stalemate possibilities, e.g. 39. P–R4, P–R4; 40. R–QR8?, R–Kt8ch; 41. K–B2, R–KB8ch, etc. There is better: 39. K–B2, P–R4; 40. R–QR8, R–Kt4; 41. R–R7, K–Kt1; 42. K–K3, R–QB4 (42. . . *R–Kt6ch; 43. K–K4, R×P; 44. R–R8ch, K–R2; 45. R–KB8 and wins*); 43. P–R4, R–Q4; 44. R–Kt7, and the threat of 45. R–Kt5, winning the Rook's Pawn, cannot be parried.

A typical Fine game. Simple methods, no direct attack, no involved combinations or complications, and yet keen motifs.

Second Illustration

Fine provides a magnificent specimen of positional play in the following game, which differs from the last in that it is his opponent who first seizes the initiative. The way in which Fine not only parries but punishes these attempts, gains the upper hand, and eventually consolidates the win is indeed memorable.

R. FINE   DR. A. ALEKHINE
White   *Black*

(Played in the Margate Easter Congress, 1937.)

DUTCH DEFENCE

1. **P–Q4, P–K3;** 2. **P–QB4, P–KB4;** 3. **P–KKt3,**

Kt–KB3; 4. **B–Kt2, B–Kt5ch;** 5. **B–Q2, B–K2;**
6. **Kt–B3, Kt–B3.**

According to the "books," the Dutch Defence is
inferior, only the Stonewall formation, which Black
could now set up by 6 . . . P–Q4, offering prospects of
equality. Experience teaches, however, that it is not
easy for White to maintain an opening advantage in
practice, since the play usually becomes very involved
and Black can threaten all sorts of dangerous attacks;
the play suits Alekhine's style, and he has indeed won
many beautiful games with this opening.

Alekhine typically rejects the quiet 6 . . . P–Q4 in
favour of the complications implied by the text move.
This time he learns a little lesson!

7.	**P–Q5!**	**Kt–K4**
8.	**Q–Kt3**	**O–O**
9.	**Kt–R3**	**Kt–Kt3**

To continue with . . . P–K4, a most important
advance for Black in this opening.

10. **P×P!**

Simple, but strong. White simultaneously opens the
Queen's file and the long diagonal, with the result that
his pieces are able to co-operate harmoniously. Experience shows that in this opening it is to Black's
benefit entirely for the centre to remain closed.

10.	. . .	**P×P**
11.	**R–Q1**	

If 11. B×P, Black would play for attack by 11 . . .
B×B; 12. Q×B, R–Kt1; 13. Q×RP, R×P. This

is stronger than 11 . . . R–Kt1; 12. B×B, R×Q; 13. B×Pch, etc., with R, B, and two Pawns for the Queen.

11. . . .   **P–B3**
12. **O–O**

To move the QB would achieve nothing.

12. . . .   **P–K4**

Far too risky. Black should have played 12 . . . K–R1 or 12 . . . Q–B2, after which, though he does have the worse of it, he retains chances of equalizing. Alekhine thinks he can permit himself aggressive tactics and thus gives Fine the opportunity of displaying his skill in positional play and defence.

13. **P–B5 dis ch**

An attacking move with positional aims, which necessitated accurate reckoning of its consequences.

13. . . .   **K–R1**
14. **Kt–KKt5**   **Q–K1**

Forced, as is his next move likewise.

15. **Kt–K6**   **B×Kt**
16. **Q×B**   **B×P**

Black has no satisfactory means of protecting his KBP, for both 16 . . . Q–B1; 17. Q×Q, QR×Q; 18. B–R3, Kt–Q2; 19. P–QKt4 (threatening 20. P–K4), and 16 . . . Kt–Q2; 17. P–QKt4, P–QR4; 18. P—QR3 would have given White an overwhelming game.

17. **Q×KBP**

This is the position White envisaged when playing 13. P–B5 dis ch. He has two Bishops and the better Pawn formation (his Pawns are in two groups, his opponent's in three). The isolated Pawn is not weak in itself, but cannot be employed for attack, and consequently Black is denied his normal chances in this opening, which consist in direct attacks on the King's side. As compensation, he has the Pawn majority on the Queen's wing, but the sequel shows he cannot exploit this owing to the power of the white Bishops.

17. . . .	R–Q1
18. Q–B2	Q–K3
19. Kt–R4	

19. Kt–K4 was also to be considered, but White does not want to exchange off either of the black Knights—they are not very mobile, anyway.

19. . . .	B–K2
20. P–QR3	

Safeguarding this Pawn and threatening 21. Kt–B5.

20. . . .	R–Q5

Averting White's threat finely. Now, if 21. Kt–B5?, then 21 . . . B×Kt; 22. Q×B, KR–Q1; 23. Q–B2, Q–Q2, and Black wins a piece.

21. **P–R3**   **P–Kt4**

Since 22. Kt—B5? would still lose a piece and the Knight must therefore return to QB3, Black considers the time ripe to start evaluating his majority on the Queen's side; but this advance, as becomes apparent later, only weakens his position still further. One or other of the quieter continuations such as 21 . . . Q–B5 or 21 . . . KR–Q1 would have been better.

22. **Kt–B3**   **P–QR4**
23. **B–K3**   **R×R**
24. **R×R**   **P–Kt5**

Black persists in his aggressive tactics, and quickly succumbs as a result. The less pretentious 24 . . . R–Q1 merited preference, but in any case White has now the better of the game.

25. **P×P**   **P×P**
26. **Kt–R4**   **Kt–Q4**
27. **B–B5!**

The two Bishops no longer mean a lot.

27. **. . .**   **Q–B2**
28. **P–K3**   **R–B1**

Losing a pawn; but Black was already at a loss for a satisfactory continuation. If, for instance, 28 . . . R–Q1, then 29. B×B winning material just the same (29 . . . Kt(Kt3)×B; 30. P–K4; or 29 . . . Q×B;

30. Q×P). Black's position is full of holes—this must prove fatal in the long run.

    29. **Q–B4**!

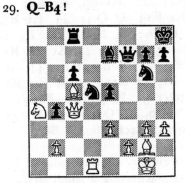

Threatening principally 30. P–K4, winning a piece. Several black Pawns are in danger, too.

    29. . . .   **Q–B1**

Nothing is much good by now, e.g. 29 . . . B×B; 30. Kt×B, R–B1; 31. R–Q2 and Black must lose a Pawn; or 29 . . . R–B1; 30. R–Q2, etc.

    30. **B×B**   **Kt(Kt3)×B**

Not 30 . . . Q×B, because of 31. B×Kt. 30 . . . Kt(Q4)×B would be answered by 31. Q×KtP.

    31. **P–K4**!   **Kt–B3**
    32. **Q×KtP**

White has picked up a Pawn and still has an overwhelming position into the bargain. The job of pushing home these big advantages we can leave to Fine. There ensued—

    32 . . . **R–Q1;** 33. **R×R, Q×R;** 34. **Kt–B5,**

Q–Q3; 35. Q–B3, P–R3; 36. Kt–Q3, Kt–Q2; 37.
P–R4, Kt–KKt3; 38. B–R3, Kt(Kt3)–B1; 39.
P–QKt4, P–R4; 40. Kt–B5, Kt–B3; 41. Q–B4,
Q–K2; 42. Kt–Kt3, Q–Q3; 43. Kt–R5, Q–Q7;
44. Kt×P, Q–K8ch; 45. B–B1, Kt×P; 46. Q–K2!
Q×Q; 47. B×Q, P–Kt3; 48, Kt×P, Kt–B6; 49.
B–Q3, K–Kt2; 50. P–B4, Kt–Q4; 51. P–Kt5,
K–B3; 52. K–B2, Kt–Kt3; 53. K–K3, Kt–R5; 54.
K–Q4, Kt–K3ch; 55. K–Q5, Kt–B2ch; 56. K–B6,
Kt–K3; 57. P–Kt6, Kt–Q1ch; 58. K–Q7, Kt–K3;
59. P–Kt7, Kt(R5)–B4ch; 60. K–B8.

Black resigns.

A model performance in the realm of logical positional play. After acquiring a small advantage in the
opening, White continually exhausted his opponent of
good moves. There are few direct threats, but, in spite
of all Black's efforts, his situation steadily deteriorates.
He missed the best line once or twice, but he was never
permitted the least chance to get back on level terms.

Third Illustration

Now follows a game which illustrates above all
Fine's combinative intrepidity.

R. FINE	W. WINTER
White	*Black*

(Played in the Nottingham tournament, 1936.)

QUEEN'S GAMBIT

1. P–Q4	P–Q4
2. P–QB4	P–QB3
3. Kt–KB3	Kt–KB3
4. P–K3	

White wants to make it as difficult for his opponent as he can, hence avoids 4. Kt–B3, which is strongest according to theory but has also been most analysed.

4. . . .		**B–B4**
5. **Kt–B3**		**P–K3**
6. **Kt–KR4**		

To avoid all chance of the game becoming drawish and to produce a difficult game, White submits to a slight delay in development to win the "minor exchange."

6. . . .	**B–K5**

6 . . . B–Kt5 was a playable alternative.

7. **P–B3**	**B–Kt3**
8. **Kt×B**	**RP×Kt**
9. **P–KKt3** !	

Because he is so strong in defence, Fine can permit himself the luxury of many variations which are superficially risky and only produce a satisfactory game with the most accurate handling. With this hardly obvious move, White forestalls all dangers along the open KR file; after 9. B–Q3, for instance, the reply 9 . . . Kt–R4 would have been rather troublesome.

9. . . .	**B–Q3**
10. **P–B4**	

The logical consequence of his preceding move. The threat was 10 . . . B×Pch, and 10. B–Kt2? would be faulty owing to 10 . . . R×P; 11. R×R, B×Pch, etc.

10. . . .	**Kt–K5**

10 . . . QKt–Q2 merited preference, whilst 10 . . .
Kt–R4 followed by 11 . . . P–KB4 and . . . Kt–B3
was also worth considering.

11. **Kt×Kt**

An important exchange. Any other move would
allow Black to get a very strong position by 11 . . .
P–KB4.

11. . . .   **P×Kt**

White has now got a mobile centre—the Queen's
Pawn being blocked no longer—and this circumstance
enhances the significance of his two Bishops. The
ensuing operations on each side are dictated by the
Pawn situation: White must work in the centre and
on the Queen's wing, Black on the King's wing—
which incidentally offers him few chances, as White
naturally does not castle on that side.

12. **B–Q2**   **Q–K2**

Probably so as to play 13 . . . B–Kt5 and exchange
off one of the white Bishops. 12 . . . Kt—Q2 would
have been better, however.

13. **P–QR3!**

One of those little moves which mark a great
master. White prevents both 13 . . . B–Kt5 and
13 . . . P–QB4, which latter would now be very
strongly met by 14. P×P, B×QBP; 15. P–QKt4.
In answer to the more obvious 13. Q–Kt3, Black would

have been able to play 13 . . . P–QB4, and continue
possibly with . . . Kt–B3 with much better chances.

13. . . .	**Kt–Q2**
14. **Q–Kt3**	

Now this move is made with gain of time.

14. . . .	**R–QKt1**

The Pawn was difficult to protect. Obviously
14 . . . O–O–O would be too dangerous. 14 . . . Kt—B3
was not quite satisfactory either, since Black could
then only with difficulty play . . . P–KB4, a move
which is required to protect the Pawn on K5.

Black's Queen's Rook is not very beautifully placed
now.

15. **Q–R4**	**P–R3**
16. **B–K2**	**P–KKt4**

This attempt to open up the King's side is, to say
the least, premature. Black should have castled.

17. **O–O–O**	**P–KB4**

Black persists in his risky tactics, advancing his
Pawns before completing his development.

18. **P×P**	

The precursor to some pretty little combinations.

18. . . .	**Q×P**

Yet again, 18. O–O would have been better.

19. **P–B5**	**B–B2**

Had Black divined his opponent's intentions, he would certainly have retreated to K2 instead, e.g. (19 . . . B–K2); 20. Q–Kt3, Q–B3; 21. B–B4, K–B2 (21 . . . *Kt–B1?* 22. *B×RP!*); but even then his situation would not have been pleasant.

20. **B×P!**

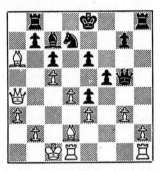

A fine and surprising move. White gets several Pawns for his piece, together with a strong King's side attack.

20. **. . .**   **P×B**

The real beauty of White's combination would have been disclosed by 20 . . . R–R1; 21. Q–Kt3!, P×B (21 . . . R×B; 22. Q×KtP, regaining the piece); 22. Q×KPch (22. *Q–Kt7, Q–Q1*) followed by 23. Q×QBP.

21. **Q×BP**

Attacking the Bishop, so that Black is compelled to leave his KP in the lurch.

21. **. . .**   **K–Q1**

There is no better continuation. In this way Black at any rate avoids the Pawn's being captured with a check.

22. Q×KP

White has already got three Pawns for his piece, among them two united passed Pawns. Another of Black's Pawns is in the air at his QR3, and his King is badly placed. Clearly White has an overwhelming game.

| 22. . . . | Q–B3 |
| 23. Q–Q5 | |

Even exchange of Queens would have been good; but the text move is much stronger, as it keeps the King's side attack going. The main threat now is 24. P–B6, regaining the piece sacrificed.

| 23. . . . | K–K2 |
| 24. B–Kt4! | |

Threatening 25. P–B6 dis ch (25 . . . R×B; 26. Q×Ktch).

| 24. . . . | KR–QB1 |

25. P—B6 dis ch would now be answered, rather neatly, by 25 . . . B–Q3!, with a promising game.

25. K–Kt1

Threatening P–B6 once again.

| 25. . . . | Kt–B1 |
| 26. P–KKt4! | |

White continually finds the strongest line.

26. . . .   **P–R4**

Not 26 . . . P×P?; 27. KR–B1 with crushing effect,
e.g. 27 . . . Q–K3; 28. Q–Kt5ch.

27. **B–B3**   **P–Kt3**
28. **P×P**   **Q×BP**

Or 28 . . . P×P; 29. QR–KB1, etc.

29. **Q–B4**   **Kt–K3**

Black is up against an impossible task, and it already
matters little how he plays.

30. **KR–B1**   **Q–R4**
31. **P–Q5**   **Kt×P**
32. **P–Q6ch!**

A pretty finish. Black resigns; mate in a few moves
is inevitable (32 . . . B×P; 33. Q–B7ch, etc.).

A charming little game. Here again Fine lays his
foundations in the very opening, but by methods quite
different from Alekhine's. Not attack, but some concrete advantage—a pair of Bishops—is his primary aim.
To achieve this he even submits to being placed on
the defensive, relying on being able to hold his own
until he is able to pass over to the attack himself—and
his confidence is vindicated.

Fourth Illustration

Fine excels in defence. He is almost unbeatable
when he gets into his stride. He has gone through
many tournaments, among them the exceptionally

strong tournaments at Nottingham in 1936 and
Semmering-Baden in 1937, without losing a game.
Flohr also scores a characteristically small proportion
of lost games, but he does not play so aggressively as
Fine and consequently does not so often have to perform
miracles of defence. The preceding game has already
revealed Fine's skill in defence. Here is a game in
which he is on the defensive throughout.

M. M. BOTVINNIK   R. FINE
White   *Black*

(Played in the Nottingham tournament, 1936.)

RETI'S OPENING

1.	Kt–KB3	P–Q4
2.	P–B4	P×P

The motif of the Queen's Gambit accepted, to which
opening Flohr, Reshevsky, and Fine are partial.

3. Kt–R3

3. P–K3, P–QB4; 4. B×P, P–K3; 5. P–Q4 would
transpose into the normal Queen's Gambit accepted,
but Botvinnik prefers modern lines.

3 . . . **P–QB4;** 4. **Kt×P, Kt–QB3;** 5. **P–QKt3,
P–B3;** 6. **B–Kt2, P–K4.**

Black has now gained the upper hand in the centre,
but on the other hand White is the better developed.
It promises to become a difficult, lively struggle.

7. **P–Kt3, KKt–K2;** 8. **B–Kt2, Kt–Q4;** 9. **O–O,
B–K2;** 10. **Kt–R4, O–O;** 11. **Q–Kt1.**

A strong move. The main threat is 12. B–K4, which
would put Black into grave difficulties since 12 . . .

P–KR3 would lose to 13. B–R7ch, and 12 . . . P–KKt3 to 13. B × KtP, P × B; 14. Q × Pch, K–R1; 15. Q–R6ch, K–Kt1; 16. Kt–Kt6, followed by P–B4, etc.

11. **. . .**   **R–B2**

Now the sacrifice on Kt6 (after 12. B–K4, P–KKt3!) would not be quite sound.

12. **Kt–B5**

This was the second idea behind 11. Q–Kt1.

12. **. . .**   **B–K3**

Many a player would have played 12 . . . B–B1 more or less automatically here, but this would have lost the exchange (13. KKt–Q6!, B × Kt; 14. B × Kt).

13. **P–B4**

Much stronger than exchanging on K7; eliminates Black's KP and re-establishes equality in the centre. It now becomes very difficult for Black, but Fine defends coolly and painstakingly.

13. **. . .**   **P × P**
14. **P × P**   **Kt–Kt3!**

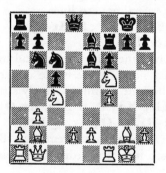

Excellently played. He threatens to win a Pawn on his QB5 or Q7. White cannot play 15. P–Q3, because that would leave the KKt unprotected; to exchange on QKt6 or K7 would weaken his attack.

15. **B–K4**!

With this fine move White sustains his attack.

15. . . .   **B × QKt**!

Again the best. After 15 . . . B × KKt or 15 . . . P–KR3 Black would soon go downhill. Nor would 15 . . . Kt × Kt be very good, because of 16. P × Kt, B × P; 17. Kt–K3! recovering the Pawn in favourable circumstances, since 17 . . . B × KP would fail against 18. R–B2, Q × P; 19. Kt–B1.

16. **P × B**   **Kt × P**
17. **B–QB3**!

Protecting the QP and threatening 18. Q × P. Black cannot continue with 17 . . . Kt × P on account of 18. QB × Kt, Q × B; 19. Q × P and wins. 17 . . . B–B1 is also unsatisfactory, e.g. 18. Kt–K3!, Kt × Kt (18. . . *Kt × P; 19. B × Pch, K–R1; 20. Q–KKt6!*, threatening 21. *Q–R5*); 19. B × Pch, K–R1; 20. P × Kt, and White's attack should win; 21. Q–KKt6 and 21. R–B3 are among the immediate threats.

17. . . .   **Kt–Q5**!

Both sides play finely. Whereas White can continually choose from among all sorts of safe continuations, Black is fighting for the draw all the time, and repeatedly has to find the one and only good move, which

makes his task much more difficult than his opponent's
and his achievement in this game a greater one.

18. Kt×Kt

After 18. B×Kt, P×B; 19. Kt×Bch, R×Kt; 20.
B×RPch, K–B1 (20 . . . *K–R1;* 21. *Q–B5!*); 21.
Q–Kt3, Q–Q4; 22. B–Kt6 (threatening 23. Q–KR3),
White's attack could hardly be stopped. But Black
has better, namely 18. B×Kt, Kt×P! Now the white
Queen is *en prise,* and 19. Kt×Bch, R×B; 20.
B×RPch, K–R1 would not essentially alter the situa·
tion. Hence the text move which, however, allows
Black to capture the QP with gain of time.

18. . . .	**P×Kt**
19. **B×RPch**	**K–B1 !**

Not 19 . . . K–R1, because of 20. B–Kt6 (20 . . .
P×B; 21. Q–B5 and wins).

20. **B–Kt4**	**P–Q6 !!**

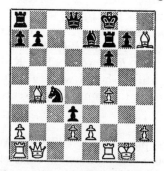

The magnificent idea behind Black's last few moves.
Black threatens to check from QKt3 and win the

Bishop, so that White has no time to go for the exchange by 21. B–Kt6.

Black thus forces a simplification in which he sheds a Pawn but gets a dead drawn position.

21. **B×Bch**

There is nothing better; let us examine, for instance, the consequences of 21. B×P, Q–Kt3ch!—

(a) 22. K–Kt2? or 22. K–R1?, B×B; 23. B×Kt, Q–B3ch; followed by 24 . . . Q×B and Black has won a piece;

(b) 22. R–B2, Q×B; 23. Q×Q, B×Q; 24. B×Kt, R–B2; and White cannot save his QP, since 25. P–Q3 is refuted by 25 . . . B–B4;

(c) 22. P–K3, Q×B; 23. Q×Q, B×Q; 24. B×Kt, R–K2!; 25. R–B2, R–Q1; 26. R–Q1, R×KP; 27. P×R, R×Rch with a drawn game.

21. . . .   **R×B**
22. **Q×QP**

The Pawn cannot be captured in any other way, because of 22 . . . Kt×P.

22. . . .   **Q×Q**
23. **P×Q**

Or 23. B×Q, Kt×P with an equal game. The text move gains a Pawn (since 23 . . . Kt×P? would lose the Knight through 24. R–B2); but what a Pawn it is! Black's position amply counterbalances such a small material advantage.

23. . . . **Kt–Kt3;** 24. **B–K4, R–Q1;** 25. **QR–B1,**

Kt–Q4; 26. **P–QR3, R(K2)–Q2;** 27. **K–Kt2, P–QKt3;** 28. **K–B3, Kt–B2.**

So as to bring the Knight to the beautiful square QB4. White must now play carefully himself so as not to fall behind.

29. **K–K3, Kt–R3;** 30. **R–QB3, Kt–B4;** 31. **R–KB2, R–Q5;** 32. **P–B5, R–R5;** 33. **R–Kt2, R(R5)–Q5.**

34. **R–KB2**

The game has come to a dead end. Neither player can undertake anything effective.

34 . . . **R–R5;** 35. **R–Kt2, R(R5)–Q5;** 36. **R–B4, R(Q5)–Q3.**

Draw agreed.

A splendid example of intrepid defence and at the same time a new illustration of Fine's skill in the handling of critical positions.

CHAPTER VIII

PAUL KERES

Keres was born on 7th January, 1916, at Narva; like Alekhine, Botvinnik, Flohr, and Reshevsky, he thus came from the old Russia. He is of Estonian nationality and now lives in Tartu.

The former Russian Baltic provinces are famous centres of chess activity and have produced a number of masters of renown—Niemtsovitch of Riga, for instance. Hence Keres grew up in surroundings which afforded plenty of chess contacts.

He was a strong player at fifteen, and only needed international experience to develop his powers. Estonia's geographical situation implies great expense to anybody who might wish to journey to other chess-playing countries, so Keres had to content himself, in the international sphere, with correspondence chess. In this he soon acquired a big reputation, his lively style attracting universal attention even in those early days. He was ready to chance any kind of gambit or bizarre opening; we even know of one correspondence game in which he opened with 1. P–KKt4. In spite of his risky style, he earned successes both in correspondence play and also in a few small tournaments on the Baltic. His career as an international tournament player began in 1935. Having won the championship of Estonia in January of that year (as the youngest of the eleven competitors) he led the national team in the International Team Tournament in Warsaw in August. He scored a pretty good result (beating

Grünfeld and Stahlberg amongst others), and the newspapers were soon talking of a rising new star.

In 1936 he participated in his first strongly contested international tournament (Bad Nauheim) with astounding success, for he tied for first place with Alekhine ahead of Bogolyubov, Stahlberg, Vidmar, van den Bosch, and four German masters. He and Alekhine each scored 6½ points out of 9 and went through the tournament unbeaten. The twenty-year-old became famous overnight. Things could not continue in this tempo. In a tournament of the same sort at Dresden a few weeks later he failed dismally, as the tournament table reveals: Alekhine 6½, Engels 6, Maroczy and Stahlberg 5½, Bogolyubov 5, Rödl and Sämisch 4½ each, Helling and Keres 3½ each, Grob ½.

In the meantime he had received an invitation to the Zandvoort tournament, and the Dutch public waited anxiously to know what he would do there. Should we see the Keres of Nauheim or the Keres of Dresden? If anything, he justified all that had been predicted of him, coming third with 6½ points out of 11, equal with Tartakover but ahead of Bogolyubov, Grünfeld, Maroczy, Spielmann, and others. He had recovered from his Dresden setback and established his reputation as an international master.

For several months little was heard of him, but when he returned in 1937, it was to make furious progress. In Margate's Easter tournament he shared first place with Fine with the good score of 7½ out of 9, each defeating Alekhine. Another tournament of ten followed immediately at Ostend. Fine and Keres started as favourites, but neither did too well; although

PAUL KERES
A brilliant challenger for the Championship

they managed to tie for first place in the end with
Grob, each totalled only 6 points. From Ostend Keres
went to Prague, where he took first place in a tournament of twelve, with 10 points (Zinner 8, Eliskases and
Foltys 7 each, etc.). After that he went on to win a
double-round tournament of four, with prescribed
openings, in Vienna; so that he returned to Estonia on
30th May loaded with fame. He left himself little time
for recuperation, for only a fortnight later the great
tournament at Kemeri in Latvia began. In this things
went none too propitiously at first, but all ended fairly
well: he shared fourth and fifth places with Alekhine,
only half a point behind Flohr, Petrov, and Reshevsky.
Three days later another tournament of eight strong
players started at Parnu in his own country. How
he would have liked to top this tournament! But
in this he was disappointed, as the score shows:
Schmidt 5½, Flohr, Keres, and Stahlberg 4½ each,
Tartakover 4, Opocensky 3½, Raud 1½, Villard 0. A
prophet is not without honour . . .? Well, Schmidt,
though German (he returned to his country after the
outbreak of the war) lived in Estonia for years and
is an "ancient" rival of Keres, whom he had already
played to a drawn match in 1935. From Parnu the
trail led to Stockholm for another International
Team Tournament, where Keres, with 11 points out
of 15, made one of the best of all the scores by top-
board players. He had now been engaged in continuous tournament play for four months, but was ready a
few days later to embark on the hardest tournament of
the year. This was the double-round tournament of
eight leading masters at Semmering-Baden, where the

result was: Keres 9, Fine 8, Capablanca and Reshevsky 7½ each, Flohr 7, Eliskases and Ragozin 6 each,
Petrov 5. Keres registered in this tournament, both
qualitatively and quantitatively, an achievement which
can only be described as grand. He won game after
game, drawing farther and farther away from the field.
With three rounds to go, he had scored 8½ points out
of 11 and stood two points ahead of his nearest rival.
Perhaps this made him a little over-confident; anyway
he lost to Eliskases and Reshevsky quite unnecessarily.
As the final result shows, he could even have allowed
himself to lose his last game to Capablanca as well,
without endangering his first prize.

He then played relatively seldom for a while.
He participated in only three events prior to the
A.V.R.O., namely the Hastings Christmas tournament (Reshevsky 7, Keres and Alexander 6½, Fine and
Flohr 6 each, Mikenas 5, etc.); a match against
Stahlberg (drawn by 2–2, with four draws); and the
tournament at Noordwijk (Eliskases 7, Keres 6, Pirc 5½,
Euwe 5, etc.). All excellent results which, however,
cannot be considered on a par with his matchless
achievement in the Semmering-Baden tournament.
Stahlberg held him in their match by consistently
going into the end-game, so cramping his combinative
powers.

The A.V.R.O. tournament provided him with yet
another resounding success, probably the greatest of
his life. From the moment he splendidly beat the then
leader Fine, at the end of the first half of the tournament, he never looked back. He had his ups and
downs—he might have lost to Euwe, to Capablanca,

to Alekhine; he threw away an easy win in his return encounter with the last named. But he always seemed able to disconcert his opponents, at a pinch, by giving the game some combinatively aggressive twist.

At Margate (Easter 1939) he collected the leading honours, ahead of Capablanca and Flohr, quite comfortably. Two of his games showed all his old brilliance, the rest he played quietly and soundly.

As we go to press, Keres has defeated Dr. Euwe by a narrow margin in a match of fourteen games; all were wild affairs of the type he revels in. This achievement finally sets the seal on his reputation.

KERES IN HIS ELEMENT

In the game which follows, Keres revives the old idea of lightning-quick, devil-may-care development, in original style.

P. KERES	W. WINTER
White	*Black*

(Played in the team tournament at Warsaw, 1935.)

SICILIAN DEFENCE

1. P–K4, P–QB4; 2. Kt–KB3, Kt–KB3; 3. P–K5, Kt–Q4; 4. Kt–B3, P–K3; 5. Kt×Kt, P×Kt; 6. P–Q4, P–Q3.

A well-known position in the Niemtsovitch variation (2 . . . Kt–KB3) of this opening. White can now isolate Black's Queen's Pawn by 7. KP×P, followed by 8. P×P, and this would give him a small positional pull; but this is a much too placid line for Keres!

7. **B–KKt5!**

The introduction to a kind of development combination, by which White, at the expense of several Pawns, brings his pieces into play with lightning rapidity.

7. . . .   **Q–R4ch**

If 7 . . . B–K2, then 8. B×B and Black must recapture with the King, otherwise a Pawn goes: 8 . . . Q×B; 9. P×BP, followed by 10. Q×P, as for example, in the game Cortlever–de Groot, Dutch championship, 1938. Equally unsatisfactory for Black is 7 . . . Q–B2; 8. P×BP, Q×P; 9. Q–Q2 (9 . . . P×P; 10. Kt×P, P–B3; 11. Kt–Q3), which leads to the isolation of Black's Queen's Pawn in circumstances very unfavourable for him.

8. P–B3

Consistent with his preceding move. 8. B–Q2, Q–Kt3; or 8. Q–Q2, Q×Qch; 9. K×Q would achieve little.

8. . . .   **BP×P**

Apparently strong, for Black would obtain a perfectly satisfactory game after either 9. Kt×P, P×P; 10. Kt–Kt3, Q–B2; 11. Q×P, B–K3; or 9. Q×P, Kt–B3.

9. B–Q3!

The first link in White's plan.

9. . . .   **P×BP**

9 . . . Kt–B3 would have been more prudent. Black possibly had not yet realized the gambit flavour the

game would assume, but believed that he was merely winning material.

10. **O–O** !

After this the stately Sicilian begins to take on the character of a Danish Gambit. White has already "lost" two Pawns, and leaves a third *en prise*.

10. . . .   **BP ✕ P**

Can Black still believe he is making all the running? Much more prudent would be 10 . . . Kt–B3; 11. R–K1, B–K3.

11. **R–Kt1**

The result of the opening skirmishes is now clear. White has developed every one of his pieces, Black only his Queen. Into the bargain, there are plenty of open files, so that the attack can start at once. All this for a mere three Pawns! The chance of Black's being able to consolidate his position before some catastrophe occurs is remote.

11. . . .   **P ✕ P**

It would, of course, be foolish to chew up the QRP as well. The text move, by which Black plans to castle as soon as possible, is also inadequate, as the white Knight gets to a powerful outpost. The only move to hold the game, even for a while, was 11 . . . Kt–B3.

12. **Kt×P**	**B–Q3**

Naturally not 12 . . . P–B3, because of 13. Q–R5ch. Black counts on 13. R–K1, O–O; 14. Q–R5, P–B4, with good chances of salvation. But things go very differently.

13. **Kt×P!**	**K×Kt**

Black has no choice.

14. **Q–R5ch**	**P–KKt3**

Some other possibilities were 14 . . . K–Kt1; 15. Q–K8ch, B–B1; 16. Q×QB and wins; or 14 . . . K–K3; 15. B–B5ch, K×B; 16. B–Q2 dis ch winning the Queen; or 14 . . . K–B1; 15. KR–K1, B–Q2; 16. R–K3 with the unmeetable threat of 17. R–B3ch.

15. **B×Pch**	**P×B**
16. **Q×R**	

Threatening simultaneously 17. Q×B and 17. Q–B6ch.

16. **. . .**	**B–KB4**
17. **KR–K1**	

Stronger than 17. Q–B6 and Q×B(Q6). 18. Q–R7ch and 19. B–R6 mate is now threatened.

17. . . .   **B–K5**
18. **R×B!**   **P×R**
19. **Q–B6ch**

Black resigns, for he is mated in a few moves, e.g.
19 . . . K–K1; 20. Q–K6ch, K–B1; 21. B–R6 mate;
or 19 . . . K–Kt1; 20. Q×Pch, K–B1; 21. Q×Bch,
etc.

A pleasing win, meritorious not for the way in
which the attack is carried through, but for White's
original construction of his game.

Second Illustration

A still better picture of Keres's very individual talent
is presented by the following wild-west game, which
opens rather irregularly, so that it is quite impossible
for Keres to have analysed in advance the complications which soon come about. In the last game he
may possibly have come prepared.

A. Dunkelblum   P. Keres
White   *Black*

(From the Ostend tournament, 1937.)

KING'S INDIAN DEFENCE

1. **P–Q4, Kt–KB3;** 2. **Kt–KB3, P–B4;** 3. **P–K3,
P–KKt3;** 4. **B–K2, B–Kt2;** 5. **O–O, O–O;** 6. **P–B4,
P–Q4.**

Both sides treat the opening irregularly, getting right
away from the books. The only thing that recalls any
theory to us is the fianchetto of Black's KB, which is
why we called the opening a King's Indian.

Obviously White is playing for a draw, but Black
wants a fight and makes for complications.

7.	**BP×P**	**Kt×P**
8.	**P×P**	**Kt–R3 !?!**

Inaugurating some horrible intricacies.

9. **B×Kt**

This exchange, which not only spoils Black's Pawn formation but also safeguards the QBP for the time being, was too tempting to forego. Needless to say, it cannot be bad; but Keres is now in his element.

9.	**. . .**	**P×B**
10.	**Kt–Q4**	

Not 10. P–K4, Kt–Kt5, after which White would get into serious trouble because of the weakness of his QB2 and Q3.

10.	**. . .**	**Q–B2**
11.	**Kt–Kt3**	**R–Q1**
12.	**Q–K2**	**P–QR4**

Looks strong. 13 . . . P–R5 is threatened, and parrying this by 13. P–QR4 would offer Black targets on the QKt file (13 . . . R–Kt1).

13. **B–Q2 !**

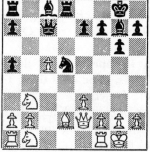

But this is apparently a complete refutation. If
Black wants to save the exchange he must leave his
Pawn on QR4 in the lurch, for 13 . . . B×P; 14.
B×P, Q–K4; 15. B×R, B×R; 16. Kt×B, Q×Kt;
17. P–K4 would not do at all, whilst 13 . . . Q–B3 (so
as to meet 14. B×P with B–QR3) would likewise be
insufficient in view of 14. Kt×P, Q×BP; 15. R–B1,
leaving White a Pawn up in a sound position.

The spectators were unanimous in thinking that
Keres was going to lose this game.

13. . . .   P–R5

Keres reveals that his position offers astounding
resources. There follow the tensest complications, and
nowhere can it be demonstrated that White should have
got definitely the better of it.

14. **B–R5**   **Q–B3**
15. **B×R**

15. Kt–Q4 would be a mistake, because of B×Kt,
16. P×B, Kt–B5!; 17. Q–B3, Kt–R6ch; 18. K–R1,
Q×Q; 19. P×Q, R×P, and Black has an overwhelming game.

15. . . .   **B–QR3**!

Hitting back—but it is not all over yet.

16. **Kt–R5**!

16. Q–Q2, B×R would be good for Black.

16. . . .   **Q–K3**!

Compare 16 . . . B×Q; 17. Kt×Q, B×R; 18.
Kt–Q2, and White has got the better of it. The text
move makes matters much more difficult for him.
Immediately after the game Keres declared that he
had expected 17. Kt–B4 as the best move and intended
to continue with 17 . . . Kt—B5! (not 17 . . . R×B;
18. QKt–R3, and Black has not sufficient compensation
for the exchange); 18. Q–B3, B×Kt!; 19. Q×R,
B–Q4!; 20. Q–Kt8!, Kt–K7ch; (the problem-like
move 20. Q–R6 fails to 21. B×P dis *ch*), 21. K–R1,
B×Pch; 22. K×B, Q–Kt5ch; 23. Q–Kt3 (forced),
Kt×Q; 24. RP×Kt, B×P; 25. Kt–Q2, B×R; 26.
R×B, Q–B1!; 27. B×P!, Q–Kt2ch; 28. P–B6!,
Q×B; 29. R–QB1. According to Keres, the game
should end in a draw then, although it is rather
dangerous for Black.

Missing this intricate salvation, White now loses
quickly.

   17. **Q–Q2?**   **B×R**
   18. **Kt–B3**

Hastening his own defeat. 18. K×B would have

been best, though White would not have been at all
enviably placed then, after 18 . . . R × B.

18. . . .	**B × P !**
19. **K × B**	**R × B**

Threatening to win the Queen.

20. **K–R1**	**P–R6 !**

A pretty finish. Black's "weak" Pawn goes on to
win the game!

21. **R–Q1**	**P × P**
22. **Kt × Kt**	**R × Kt**

White resigns, as he practically cannot stop the
Pawn from queening, e.g. 23. Q–B2, R × Rch; 24.
Q × R, Q–K5ch, etc.

"It is true that White need not have lost this game,"
Keres remarked in the *Wiener Schachzeitung*, "but it
would be unjust to a combinative player if the defending side were to see everything in the limited time
allowed for reflection."

Well does this little note reveal Keres's psychology:
he considers attacking or combining a definite achievement in itself, fully worthy of a reward. There is
indeed some truth in this.

Third Illustration

Keres does not shrink from treating front-rank international masters "*au gambit*," as the following game
shows.

P. Keres   E. Eliskases
White   *Black*

(From the tournament of eight at Semmering-Baden, 1937.)

WING GAMBIT DEFERRED

1.	P–K4	P–QB4
2.	Kt–KB3	P–Q3
3.	P–QKt4	

This development of the ordinary Wing Gambit (1. P–K4, P–QB4; 2. P–QKt4) was introduced by Keres.

3.	. . .	P×P
4.	P–Q4	Kt–KB3
5.	B–Q3	P–Q4
6.	QKt–Q2	P×P

6 . . . P–K3 was perhaps preferable.

7.	Kt×P	QKt–Q2

Preparing for . . . P–K3, which would not have been so good at this stage, because of 8. Kt×Ktch and Black must retake with the pawn, since 8 . . . Q×Kt would lose the Queen through 9. B–KKt5.

More exact than the text move would have been 7 . . . Kt×Kt; 8. B×Kt, 8. Kt–Q2.

8. Kt(K4)–Kt5!

Although this move results in the loss of several "tempi," it is strong because it confronts Black with all sorts of difficulties in development, e.g. 8 . . . P–K3 (the most natural continuation), 9. Q–K2! (threatening 10. Kt×BP, K×Kt; 11. Kt–Kt5ch, etc.), Kt–Kt3; 10. Kt–K5, Q×P; 11. R–QKt1, with a winning attack. It is therefore plausible to prepare P–K3 by P–KR3, but this would give White the opportunity of playing 9. Kt–K6! Actually, Black need not be so very much afraid of that move (9 . . . Q–Kt3!, not 9 . . . P×Kt??; 10. B–Kt6 mate), but Eliskases prefers to rule it out.

    8. . . .   **Q–B2**
    9. **P–B4**!

This surprising advance of the backward QBP, based on a tactical finesse, improves White's position a lot. It goes without saying that the Pawn phalanx Q4–QB4 is strong, and Black can hardly capture *en passant*, e.g. 9 . . . P×P; 10. Q–Kt3!, P–K3; 11. Kt×BP!, K×Kt; 12. Kt–Kt5ch, K–K1; 13. Q×KPch, B–K2; 14. Q–B7ch, K–Q1; 15. Kt–K6 mate.

9. . . .	**P–KR3**
10. **Kt–R3**	

Not 10. Kt×K4, Kt×Kt; 11. B×Kt, Q×BP.

10. . . .	**P–KKt4**

Gaining time (. . . P–Kt5 is threatened), but also producing weaknesses: Black's position is now compromised on both wings.

11. **Kt(R3)–Kt1**

Sometimes a retreat requires more courage than a sacrifice.

11. . . .	**B–Kt2**
12. **Kt–K2**	

White is a Pawn down, and half of his twelve moves have been made with the QKt (Kt–Q2; Kt×K4; Kt–Kt5; Kt–R3; Kt–Kt1; Kt–K2). Nevertheless he has a good game, thanks to his preponderance in the centre and the enfeeblement of Black's King's wing.

12. . . .	**P–K4**

Energetic. With the text move Black achieves a little success in the centre. The drawback is that the weaknesses in his position become more marked than ever.

12 . . . P–Kt3, followed by . . . B–Kt2 might have been considered.

13. **Kt–Kt3!**

Yet another move with the QKt, and an effective

one, too, for it parries . . . P–K5 and at the same time
presses on Black's weakness at his KB4.

13. ...   **O–O**
14. **O–O**   **P–K5**

Neither of the alternatives 14 . . . P×P or 14 . . .
R–K1 would get Black out of his trouble.

15. **Kt×KP**   **Kt×Kt**

The peripatetic Knight has disappeared at last.

16. **B×Kt**   **Q×BP**
17. **B–Q3**   **Q–Q4**
18. **R–K1**   **P–Kt5**

This advance would be justified only if it were to
culminate in the capture of the QP. Since this is not
the case it only means a further and very serious
weakening of Black's castled position. 18 . . . Kt–Kt3,
followed, if possible, by . . . B–B4, was indicated.

19. **Kt–R4**   **Kt–Kt3**

Black recognizes that 19 . . . Q×QP would be
sheer joy to White because of 20. R–Kt1 threatening 21.
Kt–B5 or 21. R–K4 or 21. B–Kt2, and above all 21.
B×RP (21. B×B?, B–R7ch, winning the Queen).

20. **R–Kt1**   **B–Q2**
21. **R–K4**   **KR–K1**
22. **R–B4**   **Q–Q3**

Protecting the QKtP and threatening 22 . . .
Kt–Q4, which would give Black quite a satisfactory
game.

23. **B–Q2**

Apparently attacking the QKtP again; but it immediately becomes obvious that the main idea was to provide an extra guard for the square K1.

23. . . .   **Kt–Q4**
24. **R × KKtP !**

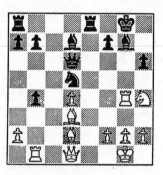

White's attack on the King's side becomes irresistible. The weaknesses in Black's castled position become painfully apparent; 18. P–Kt5 in particular proves to have been a fatal move.

24. . . .   **B × R**
25. **Q × B**

Threatening 26. Q × Bch (K × Q, 27. Kt–B5ch). We see why White played 23. B–Q2: 25 . . . R–K8ch had to be prevented, otherwise the immediate sacrifice of the exchange would have been still stronger.

25.	. . .	**Q–B3**
26.	**Kt–B5**	**K–B1**
27.	**Kt × B**	**Q × Kt**
28.	**Q–R5**	**Kt–B3**

Black's moves are forced all the time.

29.	Q–R4	P–KR4
30.	R×P	QR–B1
31.	P–KR3	R–B2
32.	R–Kt5	R–K3

Loses at once, but Black was hopelessly placed any-way, since he had no compensation whatever for the very bad position of his King. Tarrasch has pointed out that a Rook and two Bishops are usually stronger than two Rooks and a Knight. Here White possesses a strong extra Pawn and all sorts of positional advantages as well.

33. R×RP!

Black resigned, for 33 . . . Kt×R would be answered by 34. Q–Q8ch, R–K1; 35. B–Kt4ch and mate in three. A pretty finish. When we recall how very strong is Eliskases in defence (as, for instance, the great attacking player Spielmann discovered to his sorrow in no fewer than three matches), then we get an idea how tremendous was Keres's achievement in this game.

Fourth Illustration

Here is an encounter in which Keres attacks violently by purely positional means.

P. KERES	S. FLOHR
White	*Black*

(From the tournament of eight at Semmering-Baden, 1937.)

KING'S INDIAN DEFENCE

1. **P–Q4, Kt–KB3;**   2. **P–QB4, P–KKt3;**   3. **Kt–KB3, B–Kt2;**   4. **P–KKt3, P–B3;**   5. **B–Kt2, P–Q4;**   6. **P×P, Kt×P.**

6 . . . P×P is safer, producing a symmetrical position in which White has gained practically no opening advantage.

7. **O–O!**

7. P–K4 turned out very badly in the game Fine–Reshevsky, Kemeri, 1937: 7. P–K4 ,Kt–Kt3; 8. O–O, B–Kt5; 9. B–K3, P–QB4!, and White got into great difficulties.

7 . . . **O–O;** 8. **Kt–B3, Kt×Kt;** 9. **P×Kt, P–QB4;** 10. **B–QR3, P×P.**

10 . . . Kt–R3 or 10 . . . Kt–Q2 would have been better.

11. **Kt×P!**

Much stronger than 11. P×P. White allows his Pawn position to be weakened, but every one of his pieces develops the fullest activity—and exploiting this sort of advantage is just what Keres likes.

11. . . .   **Q–B2**

In this open position Black dare not go for the majority of Pawns on the Queen's side by 11 . . . B×Kt, of course, because it would leave White with two dangerous Bishops. White's game is as overwhelming after 12. Q×B as after 12. P×B.

12. **Q–Kt3**   **B–B3**

Preparing . . . Kt–Q2. Black wants to maintain the
better Pawn formation, so avoids 12 . . . Kt–B3, after
which White would acquire a small but definite opening
advantage by Kt×Kt.

13.	**KR–Q1**	**Kt–Q2**
14.	**P–QB4!**	

The "weak" Pawn is going to join in the attack, and
shows plenty of healthiness. Black has to reckon with
the possibility of P–B5 and P–B6.

14.	. . .	**Kt–B4**
15.	**Q–Kt4**	**Kt–K3**
16.	**Kt–Kt5**	**Q–K4**
17.	**QR–B1**	

White's last moves have been nicely calculated, the
point being that the KP cannot now be captured:
17 . . . Q×KP; 18. Kt–B3!, Q–R4 (or 18 . . . *B×Kt;*
19. *Q×B*, with an irresistible attack); 19. Kt–Q5,
R–K1; 20. Q–Kt5, and White has a big pull positionally. Black is in trouble.

17.	. . .	**R–Q1**
18.	**R–Q5!**	

Magnificently played. If Black now captures the
King's Pawn, there would follow: 19. R–K1, Q×RP;
20. R×Rch, Kt×R; 21. R×P!, B×R; 22. Q×B,
Q–R8ch; 23. B–KB1, Kt–K3; 24. Kt–B7, R–Kt1;
25. Q–K8ch, K–Kt2; 26. Kt×Ktch, B×Kt; 27.
B–B8ch, K–B3; 28. Q×R and wins (28 . . . *B×P;*
29. *Q–B4ch* or 28 . . . *B–R6;* 29. *Q–Q6ch, K–B4;* 30.
Q–Q7ch).

Since 18 . . . Q–Kt1 would be powerfully countered by 19. R(B1)–Q1 Blacks finds himself compelled to dissolve White's Pawn-position weakness after all by exchanging on Q4.

18. . . .	R×R
19. P×R	P–QR3

Bad execution of a sound idea. Black should have attacked the Knight, not with the Pawn but with the Bishop. After 19 . . . B–Q2; 20. Kt–B3 (20. *P×Kt*, *B×Kt*), Kt–Q1, the position, whilst admittedly very difficult for Black, would have been far from lost.

The text move finds a charming refutation.

20. **Kt–R7!!**

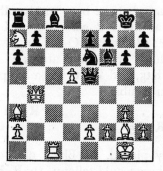

An astonishing continuation, with which White forces the win of a piece. If Black captures the Knight, he loses a Rook after 21. R×Bch, Kt–B1; 22. Q–Kt6, whilst 20 . . . B–Q2 fails to 21. P×Kt and 20 . . . Kt–B2 to 21. Kt×B, R×Kt; 22. Q×KtP. It is "all over bar shouting."

20 . . . Kt–Q5; 21. R×Bch, R×R; 22. Kt×R, Q×KP; 23. P–R4, Kt–B4; 24. Q–K4.

Black resigns, for neither exchange of Queens nor 24 . . . Q×RP, 25. Kt×Pch offers any hope.

It has been a clash between two widely diverging conceptions, Keres representing the strategy of the middle-game, Flohr that of the end-game. The man who lives in the present beats the one who lives for the future—it is nothing new!

Fifth Illustration

Finally, a game which presents Keres as an end-game artist.

S. Reshevsky
White

P. Keres
Black

(From the Semmering-Baden tournament, 1937.)

QUEEN'S INDIAN DEFENCE

1. Kt–KB3, Kt–KB3; 2. P–B4, P–K3; 3. P–Q4, P–QKt3; 4. P–KKt3, B–Kt2; 5. B–Kt2, B–Kt5ch; 6. B–Q2, B×Bch; 7. Q×B, O–O; 8. O–O, P–Q3; 9. Q–B2, QKt–Q2; 10. Kt–B3, Q–K2; 11. P–K4.

White has slightly the better of it. In this opening it is most important for Black to impede or nullify White's P–K4. Keres has neglected this, probably on purpose, so as to confuse the struggle.

11. . . .		QR–B1 !
12.	KR–K1	P–K4
13.	QR–Q1	

13. Kt–Q5 would be answered by Kt × Kt followed by P–QB3—this explains 11 . . . R–B1.

13.	. . .	P–B3
14.	Q–R4	

White fails to produce a useful plan. It was correct to move the Queen, as she was unsatisfactorily posted on the same file as Black's Rook; but 14. Q–Q2 (perhaps preceded by Kt–KR4) was to be preferred.

14.	. . .	R–B2
15.	Q–R3	R–K1
16.	P–Kt3	P–Kt3
17.	P × P	

White over-estimates the importance of the square Q6. The text move, which leads to an exchange of Queens, produces an end-game in which White's present advantage, his command of a little more space, slowly disappears; consequently the weakness on his Q4 becomes of more moment than the one on Black's Q3.

17 . . . P × P; 18. Q × Q, R × Q; 19. B–R3, B–B1; 20. P–QKt4, Kt–B1; 21. B × B, R × B; 22. R–Q6, Kt–K1; 23. R–Q3, P–B3; 24. R(K1)–Q1, K–B2; 25. P–QR4.

A vain attempt to obtain some tangible target, but this rushing forward the Pawns on the Queen's wing only enfeebles White's position.

25 . . . K–K3; 26. R–Q8, R(K2)–QB2!; 27. K–B1, K–K2.

Black's weaknesses on the Q file have disappeared,

and Keres soon succeeds in fully re-establishing the
equilibrium on this file.

28. **R(Q8)–Q3, R–Q2;** 29. **R × Rch, Kt × R ;** 30.
K–K2, Kt–Q3 ; 31. **Kt–Q2, Kt–B1 !**

Aiming for Q5. Black now takes the lead.

| 32. **R–QR1** | **Kt–K3** |
| 33. **P–R5** | |

White can hardly remain completely passive; yet
his efforts to attack on the Queen's wing have no
satisfactory outcome and Black's advantage becomes
clearer and clearer.

| 33. **. . .** | **P–QKt4 !** |
| 34. **P × P** | |

After 34. P–B5, Kt–Q5ch; 35. K–Q3, Kt–B2;
followed by . . . R–Q1 and possibly . . . Kt–Kt4 and
. . . Kt(Kt4)–K3, it is Black who invades along the
Queen's file. The text move too has its drawbacks (it
opens the file of Black's Rook), but White at least
obtains some prospects of counter-play along the QB
or Q file.

34 . . . **Kt–Q5ch ;** 35. **K–Q3, P × P ;** 36. **R–B1,
K–K3 ;** 37. **Kt–K2.**

White's intention with 34. P × P is now evident:
simplification and a draw.

| 37. **. . .** | **Kt–B3 !** |

Forcing the white Rook to leave the QB file. See
how the enfeeblement of White's Queen's wing is
helping Black to get the upper hand.

| 38. **R–QKt1** | **R–Q1 !** |

Preparing to push forward in the centre. Black wants to force the white King to make up his mind: if 38. K–K3, then after 39 . . . Kt–B5ch the Queen's file becomes a most important base of operations. Hence White's reply.

39.	**K–B3**	**P–B4**!

Black is gaining more and more ground. The text move leaves White no choice, for 40. P–B3 would be answered by P×P, 41. P×P, R–KB1 (42. R–KB1, Kt×KPch); or if 41. Kt×P, Kt×Ktch; 42. P×Kt, R–KB1; and the Rook penetrates into White's position.

40.	**P×Pch**	**P×P**
41.	**P–B3**	**R–QB1**
42.	**K–Q3**	**Kt–K1**!

The effect of his operations in the centre: the square Q4 is now available for a Knight.

43.	**Kt–B3**	**Kt–B3**!

If now 44. Kt×P, then 44 . . . Kt–Q4, and both White's Queen's-side Pawns soon fall.

44.	**R–Kt2**	**P–QR3**
45.	**P–Kt4**	

White has a bad game, and he can hardly make anything of passive defence in the long run. His Queen's wing is weak, he is cramped in the centre, and finally he is threatened with an action on the King's wing, commencing with a break-through by P–R4 and P–R5 and sustained by the invasion of the

Rook along the Knight's or Rook's file. The text move, dictated by necessity, is an endeavour to confuse the issue, e.g. 45 . . . P×P; 46. P×P, Kt×KKtP; 47. Kt(Q2)-K4, R-Q1ch; 48. K-B2 threatening 49. Kt-B5ch or 49. Kt-Kt5ch. The loss of his QRP might cause serious trouble for Black.

45. . . .   **P-K5ch!**

A beautiful break-through, with which Black refutes the counter-action and increases his advantage decisively.

The point of this move is revealed in the subsequent course of the game: Black can always get a passed Pawn out of the majority he now obtains on the King's wing, and the advance of this Pawn finally proves irresistible.

46. **BP×P**

Forced, for 46. K-B2 or 46. K-K2 would fail against 46 . . . Kt-Q5ch, whilst 46. K-K3 can be met by 46 . . . Kt×QKtP or even 46 . . . Kt-K2!

46 . . . Kt–K4ch!; 47. K–B2, P×KtP; 48. K–Kt3, Kt–B5!; 49. Kt×Kt.

Again forced; e.g. 49. R–B2, Kt×Ktch; 50. R×Kt, R×Kt!; 51. K×R, Kt×Pch, etc.

49 . . . R×Kt; 50. R–K2, K–K4; 51. R–K1, P–R4!

Much stronger than capturing the KP at once. Black gets a passed Pawn on the King's Knight'ᵉ file, and the win is then easy.

52. R–Q1, P–R5; 53. R–Q8, P–Kt6; 54. P×P, P×P; 55. R–Q3, P–Kt7!

Now 56. R–Kt3 is out of the question, because of R×Ktch!, etc.

56. Kt–K2, R×KP; 57. Kt–Kt1, R–K8!

White resigns, since 58. Kt–B3ch is of no avail.

A first-rate achievement in the realm of end-play.

CHAPTER IX

DR. MACHGIELIS EUWE

Dr. M. Euwe was born at Watergraafsmeer on 20th May, 1901. It was his mother who instructed him in the first rudiments of chess. At the early age of ten he participated in a one-day Christmas congress at Amsterdam and won every game; but he was never launched forth as an infant prodigy.

His chess talents gradually developed, albeit at no expense to his studies, and by 1920 he had already become the leading figure in Dutch chess. A year later he opened his annual subscription to the title of Dutch champion and played Maroczy to a draw in a private match (2 wins each, with 8 draws). He subsequently made several successful incursions into foreign chess congresses.

He gained his Doctorate in 1926, and in December–January 1926–7 achieved his first sensational success, losing a match to Alekhine by the extremely small margin of 2 games to 3 (with 5 draws). In 1928 he was twice defeated by Bogolyubov, though again by the narrowest of margins (2–3 with 5 draws; and 1–3 with 7 draws). These were great achievements for a pure amateur, and the world rightly acclaimed them as such.

In 1930 he scored a resounding success at Hastings, topping the Premier section ahead of Capablanca, who, however, defeated him in a subsequent match by 2–0 with 8 draws. 1932 was a good year. He beat Spielmann by 2–0 with 2 draws and drew two matches with Flohr, with whom he shared second place in a tournament at Berne behind Alekhine.

Then came a break in his chess career through his devoting himself to his mathematical studies for a while. Alekhine's slight lapse in the Christmas tournament at Hastings 1933–4 suddenly gave him the idea of challenging the now world champion to another match, and by the summer of 1935 the great event had been arranged.

In the meantime he scored two more successes, sharing second place with Flohr behind Alekhine once again, this time at Zurich, and winning the Christmas tournament at Hastings, in company with Sir George Thomas and Flohr, ahead of Capablanca, Lilienthal, and Botvinnik.

The dramatic result of his first match against Alekhine is old history. Three points down after seven games, he pulled up to equality, only to see his redoubtable opponent draw away again. Battling gamely, he was still two down at the two-thirds stage, but won the twentieth, twenty-first, twenty-fifth, and twenty-sixth games and retained his grip on a now desperate adversary to the end.

Euwe's great characteristic is economy of force. He is logic personified, a genius of law and order. His play is accurate and aggressive. One would hardly call him an attacking player, yet when his genius is functioning at its smoothest he strides confidently into some extraordinarily complex positions: he is no disciple of simplicity.

His great weakness is a tendency to blunder. Kmoch asks: "Has he some psychological antipathy to real-

Dr. "Max" Euwe
World Champion 1935-7

ism? I am no psychologist, and cannot say. The fact remains that Euwe commits the most inexplicable mistakes in thoroughly favourable positions, and that this weakness has consistently tarnished his record."

His winning the world title stimulated him to some brilliant results during 1936, results which, even though blemished by blunders, bear comparison with those of any world champion before or since. Blunders alone cost him first place at Zandvoort and Nottingham and a better standing among the first-board masters in the Stockholm Olympiad.

However, in two very strongly contested tournaments played at various localities in Holland and Germany respectively, he topped the list, above Alekhine on each occasion. When the return match for the world championship began, he could look back with satisfaction on two wins and a draw as the outcome of their last three encounters, and he added a further win in the first game of the match.

Then the tide gradually began to turn against him; we have gone into some of the possible reasons. The temporary loss of his "second," Reuben Fine, through appendicitis, was a sad blow, for Fine collaborated in opening and adjournment analysis, and it is an undeniable fact that a great part of Alekhine's success was due to the almost miraculous analysis that he put into several positions on adjournment in co-operation with his second, Eliskases. Adding this factor to Euwe's commission of even more serious blunders than usual, one is bound to regard the final margin of five points against him as a tremendous exaggeration of the real difference between the players.

He could only reach fourth place in one subsequent Dutch tournament, but was terribly handicapped through carrying on with his teaching duties throughout, working all day and playing in the evenings. For the A.V.R.O. tournament he had inadequate preparation, and only received leave of absence at the very last moment. This probably went far to account for his depressing start; in the second half of the tournament, however, he staged a "come-back" which delighted his supporters and must have restored all his self-confidence, beating Fine, Botvinnik, and Capablanca (the latter for the first time in his life), and drawing his remaining four games. He faltered a little in the 1938-9 Christmas congress at Hastings, losing to Landau and finishing behind Szabo, but he has since scored a fine "first" in a Dutch tournament above Flohr, Szabo, and Landau, and has annexed the Dutch championship twice again. His latest achievement is to crush the strong player Landau mercilessly by 5-0 with 5 draws in a match for the Dutch championship.

The foundation of Euwe's success is undoubtedly his deep knowledge of opening theory. Here are two games which illustrate this.

ENGAGES THE ENEMY

First Illustration

DR. M. EUWE   S. FLOHR
White   *Black*

(From the tournament of six, Amsterdam, 1939.)

QUEEN'S GAMBIT, SLAV DEFENCE

1.	P–Q4	P–Q4
2.	P–QB4	P–QB3
3.	Kt–KB3	Kt–B3
4.	Kt–B3	P–KKt3

An unusual "modulation" from the Slav Defence to the Grünfeld, which, by the way, is not too favourable, since the passive move . . . P–QB3 is, as a rule, only satisfactory when White has shut in his QB by P–K3.

5.	B–B4	B–Kt2

In a match game between the same adversaries (1932) 5 . . . P×P; 6. P–QR4, Kt–Q4; 7. B–Q2, Kt–Kt5 was played, and Black got the better of it. Subsequent analysis showed that it should be White who obtains the best prospects after 6. P–K3 (instead of P–QR4), e.g. P–QKt4; 7. P–QR4, Kt–Q4; 8. P×P, Kt×Kt; 9. P×Kt, P×P; 10. Q–Kt1! regaining the Pawn.

6.	P–K3	O–O

The drawback to Black's method is apparent: if he wants to make the natural riposte to B–KB4 in the Grünfeld Defence, namely . . . P–QB4, his second move would turn out to have been a mere waste of time.

7.	Q–Kt3	P×P

He can hardly continue his development otherwise.

8.	B×P	QKt–Q2
9.	Kt–K5	Q–K1

Useless, as soon becomes clear. 9 . . . Kt×Kt at once was to be preferred.

  10. **B–K2**

Preventing . . . Kt–R4.

  10. . . .   **Kt×Kt**
  11. **B×Kt**   **Q–Q1**
  12. **O–O**

Partly as a result of Black's weak ninth move, White has now by far the better prospects.

  12. . . .   **Q–Kt3**

So as to develop his QB, which has been tied down to the defence of the QKtP.

  13. **Q–R3**   **R–K1**
  14. **QR–B1**   **B–B1**

A scarcely natural move, with which Black wastes more valuable time. With 14 . . . P–QR4, followed by . . . Q–Kt5, he could still have got a reasonable game. Not, however, 14 . . . B–K3; 15. Kt–R4 and Kt–B5.

  15. **Kt–R4**   **Q–Q1**
  16. **KR–Q1**

White has played the opening in his characteristically clean-cut way, to obtain a tremendous advantage in development.

  16. . . .   **Kt–Q4**
  17. **P–K4**   **P–K3**

He must get in this move at once, since 17 . . .

Kt–Kt3 could have been very strongly met by 18. P–Q5. But now the luckless QB is imprisoned behind its own Pawns.

18. **Q–KB3**

Probably better than 18. Q–KKt3, Kt–B3, etc.

| 18. . . . | **Kt–Kt3** |
| 19. **Kt–B5** | **Kt–Q2** |

A rather neat little manœuvre which forces off a couple of pieces without wasting time, but also without improving Black's situation a lot.

| 20. **Kt × Kt** | **B × Kt** |
| 21. **B–B6** | |

Note the remorseless logic: White methodically completes his development before making any offensive overtures, but the moment the time is ripe he moves to the attack.

| 21. . . . | **Q–R4** |

With 21 . . . B–K2; 22. P–K5 Black would have

left himself fatally weak on the black squares round his King.

22. R–B5!

The Rook is untouchable, since Black would lose two Bishops for it; 22 . . . B×R; 23. P×R, and Black must leave the QB *en prise* in view of the threat Q–K3–R6.

| 22. . . . | Q×P |
| 23. R–KR5! | P–K4 |

Black must hold up Q–KR3 at all costs. Another way of doing this was 23 . . . Q×P, which would have transposed back to the actual game. On the other hand, 23 . . . B–Kt2 would lose: 24. B×B, K×B; 25. R×Pch, K×R; 26. Q×Pch, K moves; 27. R–Q3, Q–Kt8ch; 28. B–B1, P–K4; 29. Q×B, etc.

| 24. P×P | B–K3 |

Black has to waste a move with his attacked Bishop, but he has more defensive resources than appear on the surface.

| 25. Q–B4 | Q×P |
| 26. B–B1 | |

26. B–B3 would have been better. Now Flohr manages to confuse the issue a little.

| 26. . . . | B–K2 |

Not 26 . . . B–Kt2; 27. B×B and wins as before.

27. Q–R4

If 27. Q–R6, then B×B; 28. P×B, Q×P(B3). The Queen is doing quite useful work—so White might

well have tried to undermine her position on QKt7 by
27. R–Kt1!, Q–Q5 (27 . . . *Q×R?*; 28. *Q–R6, etc.*);
28. R–Kt4!!, Q–R8; 29. Q–R4!, and White wins,
since Black's occupation of the seventh rank, which
proved so valuable in the actual game, is eliminated.

27. . . .   **B–QB4!**

Very well played. 28. R × P is prevented because of
28 . . . Q × BPch, and if 29. K–R1, Q–Kt8 mate. Had
the white Bishop gone to B3 on the twenty-sixth move,
this variation would not have been possible.

28. **R–R6**   **P–R4**

It suddenly looks as if Black might—win!

29. **R–Q3**   **B × Pch**

Forced, for 30. R–KB3 (protecting KB2) followed
by R × P was threatened. 29 . . . B–B5 would be no
defence: 30. R × P, Q × BPch; 31. Q × Q, B × Qch;
32. K × B, K × R; 33. R–KR3ch, and mate next move.

30. **Q × B**   **Q × Qch**
31. **K × Q**   **P–R5**

How is White going to neutralize the menacing onrush of the Pawns?

32. **B–K2 !**

This beautifully quiet move is the solution. White is going to screen his KR3 for use by a Rook, by 33. P–Kt4. This leaves Black no time to queen his Rook's Pawn, the whole point being that White threatens not 33. P—Kt4, 34. R(Q3)–KR3, and 35. R×P, but 33. P–Kt4 and 34. R×P at once, which saves a vital move. It seems a matter of touch and go but is not so in reality as Euwe has every eventuality neatly docketed.

32. . . .	**R–R4**
33. **P–Kt4**	**R×P**

Desperation; otherwise 34. R×P would finish the game at once.

34. **B×R**	**B–B5**
35. **R(Q3)–KR3**	**B×B**
36. **B–B6**	**R–K3**

If 36 . . . R×P; 37. R×RP, R–B5ch; 38. K×B, R×B; 39. R–R8ch and mate.

37. **P–K5**	**B×P**
38. **R×RP**	**R×Bch**
39. **P×R**	

Black resigns, for his passed Pawns can now be easily stopped: 39 . . . B×R; 40. R×B, P–QKt4; 41. R–QB3, P–Kt5; 42. R×P, P–Kt6; 43. R–Kt6, etc., or 40 . . . P–B4; 41. R–QB3, P–Kt3; 42. R–B4, P–R6; 43. R–QR4.

A game like a detective novel, with an unexpected *dénouement* on the thirty-second move.

Second Illustration

DR. M. EUWE   L. SZABO
White   *Black*

Q.G.D., HALF-SLAV DEFENCE

(From the tournament of six, Amsterdam, 1939.)

1.	P–Q4	P–Q4
2.	P–QB4	P–QB3
3.	Kt–KB3	Kt–B3
4.	Kt–B3	P–K3

A much keener variation than it appears to be. In the first place White has to shut in his QB, since 5. B–Kt5, P–KR3 would force him to give up the minor exchange by 6. B×Kt, *not* 6. B–R4, P×P; 7. P–R4, B–Kt5; followed by . . . P–QKt4, and White cannot recover the Pawn.

5.	P–K3	B–K2

Avoiding the Meran defence (5 . . . QKt–Q2; 6. B–Q3, P×P; 7. B×BP, P–QKt4; 8. B–Q3, P–QR3; followed by . . . P–B4) in favour of an old and rather passive line.

6.	B–Q3	O–O
7.	O–O	P×P

It would be better to stick to his original plan and complete his development by 7 . . . P–QKt3, B–Kt2, etc., before thinking of complications. The text move

could still lead to a Meran defence position but Black
has wasted valuable time, through playing 5 . . . B–K2
instead of 5 . . . QKt–Q2, as would be evident if the
following variation were adopted—

8. B×P, P–QKt4; 9. B–Q3, P–QR3; 10. P–K4,
P–B4; 11. P×P!, B×P; 12. P–K5, Kt–Q4; 13.
Kt–K4, B–K2; 14. B–Kt5, etc.

However, Black has quite other intentions.

8.	**B×P**	**P–QKt4**
9.	**B–Q3**	**P–Kt5?**

Indeed a naïve mistake for a master of this class.
The QBP now becomes permanently weak, and White
can put it under fire in a variety of ways. The fact
that Black now decides to complicate the game proves
that the combination of 5 . . . B–K2 and 6 . . . O–O
with 7 . . . P×P is doubtful.

This whole scheme is an invention of A. Steiner. It
is not easy to refute a prepared variation, even a bad
one! But it is very doubtful whether the variation is
new to Euwe and he knows just what to do.

10.	**Kt–QR4**	**B–R3**

Neither 10 . . . Kt–R3; 11. Q–B2, Q–B2; 12.
B–Q2 (12 . . . P–B4; 13. P×P; and 14. R–B1) nor
10 . . . QKt–Q2; 11. Q–B2, Q–R4; 12. B–Q2! would
enable Black to get in the so essential . . . P–B4, in
the latter case because of (12 . . . P–B4) 13. P–QR3
(threatening 14. *Kt×P* and 15. *P×P*), BP×P; 14.
Kt×P, B–Kt2; 15. P×P, KB×P; 16. Kt–Kt3!, etc.

11.	**Kt–K5**

Threatening Kt×QBP. If Black wants to develop his Queen's wing he has nothing better than to exchange the Bishops, enabling White to strengthen the pressure on QB5.

11.	. . .	B×B
12.	Kt×B	QKt–Q2
13.	B–Q2	P–QR4
14.	R–B1	

Crystal-clear strategy!

14.	. . .	R–B1
15.	P–B3	

15. Q–B3 looks attractive; but is not so good, because of 15 . . . P–B4!; 16. P×P, Kt×P! With the text move White plans P–K4 and B–K3, after which his position would not be far from ideal.

15.	. . .	Kt–Kt3

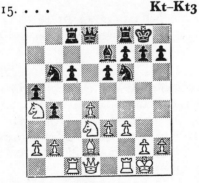

16. **Kt–K5!**

Refuting Black's whole plan; even stronger than 16. Kt(R4)–B5. The QBP is lost, for the black Queen

cannot guard both the Knight and the attacked Pawn,
whilst 16 . . . Kt×Kt; 17. Q×Kt, P–B4 fails against
18. Kt–B6, Q moves; 19. Kt×Bch, Q×Kt; 20.
Q×RP, etc.

16. . . .	**P–B4**
17. **Kt×QBP**	**B×Kt**
18. **P×B**	**Q–Q4**

18 . . . Kt(Kt3)–Q2 would have been a little better;
19. Kt–Q3!, Kt–Kt1; 20. Q–B2, but any attempt to
regain the Pawn by 20 . . . Q–Q4 (threatening R–Q1)
would fail through 21. Kt–B4! (21 . . . Q×RP; 22.
R–R1, etc.).

19. **P×Kt**	**Q×Kt**
20. **R×R**	**R×R**
21. **P–Kt7**	**R–Q1**

Or 21 . . . R–Kt1; 22. Q–B1!, P–R3; 23. P–K4,
P–Kt4; 24. Q–B6, followed by B–K3 and B–R7.

22. **P–K4?**

At this critical stage White succumbs to a characteristic lapse and manages to give back his Pawn for
nothing, in the simplest way. After 22. Q–B1, the
game would have been over in a few moves.

(i) 22 . . . P–R3; 23. Q–B8, Q–Kt1; 24. R–B1,
K–R2; 25. Q–B7!, etc.

(ii) 22 . . . Q–Kt1; 23. Q–B6!, R×B (otherwise
White retains the Pawn); 24. R–B1 (threatening
25. *Q–B8ch, R–Q1;* 26. *Q×Q, R×Q;* 27. *R–B8ch*),
R–Q1; 25. Q–R6! and wins through the threat of

R–B8, since 25 . . . Q–K4 fails against 26. R–B8, Q×KPch; 27. K–B1, and Black cannot check again.

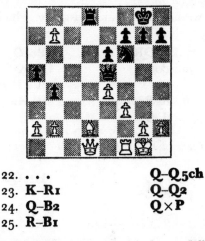

22. . . .	Q–Q5ch
23. K–R1	Q–Q2
24. Q–B2	Q×P
25. R–B1	

Now a very difficult game develops. White commands more of the board, a circumstance which makes his Bishop stronger than Black's Knight. Black's advanced Pawns on the Queen's side deter him from exchanging Queens, since their weakness would then become fatal; this very inability to allow exchange of Queens causes him a lot of trouble in view of White's possession of the QB file. Euwe handles this part of the game with splendid accuracy.

25. . . .	P–R3
26. B–K3	Q–Kt4
27. K–Kt1	R–Q6
28. K–B2	P–Kt6?

Promoting the very exchange he should have avoided.

He could have put up a better resistance by a waiting move such as 28 . . . R–Q1 (29. Q–B5, Q–R5 or 29. Q–B6, Q–R4).

Dr. Euwe now forces an end-game, which is, rather curiously, a clear-cut win.

29.	**P–QR4!**	**P×Q**
30.	**P×Q**	**R–Kt6**
31.	**R×P**	**R×P(Kt4)**
32.	**R–B8ch**	**K–R2**
33.	**B–Q4**	

The threats of R–QR8 and B–B3 now cost Black the game.

33.	**· · ·**	**Kt–Q2**
34.	**R–B7**	

If 34. R–QR8 at once, then 34 . . . Kt—B4; 35. B–B3, P–R5, etc.

34.	**· · ·**	**Kt–K4**
35.	**K–K2**	

Not, of course, 35. B×Kt, R×B; 36. R×P, R–QKt4.

35.	**· · ·**	**K–Kt3**
36.	**P–B4**	

Eradicating the possibility of Kt–B3 (e.g. after 36. R–R7?).

36.	**· · ·**	**Kt–Kt5**
37.	**B–B3**	

Simply 37. P–R3, Kt–B3; 38. K–K3, Kt–K1; 39.

R–Q7, followed by B–B3 and R–R7 would have been good enough.

Or 37 . . . P–K4; 38. B–B3, Kt–B3; 39. K–B3, P×P; 40. K×P followed by R–R7.

In another master this move would have been dismissed as a mere flourish, but such a gesture is quite foreign to Euwe. It is merely that he sees he can force a distant passed Pawn which, with the far-striding Bishop against Knight, *must*, according to his beloved principles, win. So he marches for this theoretically won position by the most direct way.

37. . . .	Kt×P
38. R–R7	Kt–Kt5
39. R×RP	R×R

If he leaves the Rooks on, the procedure will be P–Kt4, P–Kt5, B–Q4, P–Kt6, R–R7, etc.

40. B×R	P–B4

The King could not march along the rank at once, since 40 . . . K–B3 would be answered simply by 41. B–Q8ch; or 40 . . . P–K4; 41. P–B5ch, K–B3??; 42. B–Q8 mate!!

White's passed Pawn dominates the rest of the game.

41. P–Kt4, Kt–B3; 42. P–Kt5, Kt×P; 43. B–Kt4, momentarily stalemating the Knight. 43 . . . Kt–B3; 44. P–Kt6, Kt–Q2; 45. P–Kt7, K–R4; 46. B–Q6, K–Kt5; 47. K–Q3, K–R4; 48. K–B4, K–Kt3; 49. K–Kt5, K–B2; 50. K–B6, K–K1.

51. **B–B8!**, P–Kt4; 52. **B×P**, P×P; 53. **B×P,
P–K4;** 54. **B–Kt5,** Kt–Kt1ch; 55. **K–Q6,** P–K5;
56. **K–K5,** Kt–R3; 57. **K×P,** K–Q2; 58. **B–B4,
P–K6;** 59. **P–Kt8(Q).**

Black resigns.

Third Illustration

E. Klein   Dr. M. Euwe
White   *Black*

(From the Congress at Hastings, 1938–9.)

The Bishops on oppositely coloured squares make
the draw almost inescapable.

Black decides this very difficult ending by means of
a most striking combination about twelve moves deep.
The leitmotifs of the position are—

(1) Black wins if he can get two connected passed
Pawns.

(2) Black wins if he can get a Pawn majority on
each wing.

| 30. . . . | **B–B3** |

Threatening 31 . . . R–K7ch and practically forcing
White's reply.

31. **R–K1**	**P–Q7**
32. **R–Q1**	**R–K5**
33. **B–K5**	

White is repeatedly denied all choice of moves.
After 33. R×P, R×Pch White would lose either the
QRP or the KtP as well.

33. . . .	**R–R5**
34. **B–Q6**	**R–Q5**
35. **B–B5**	

White had to attack the Rook, since 35 . . . B–R5
was threatened, and after 35. B–K5, R–Q6 the QRP
falls.

| 35. . . . | **R×Pch** |
| 36. **K–K3** | |

If 36. K–Kt3, then 36 . . . R–B6ch; 37. K–R4,
P–KR3; 38. P–Kt5, B–Q2, and White is mated.

| 36. . . . | **R×P** |
| 37. **B×P** | |

Now it seems as if White draws easily, since the QP
goes; but we have not seen half of the combination
yet.

| 37. . . . | **R–KR5!** |
| 38. **B–Kt8** | |

The only way to save both Pawns.

38. . . .	**R–R6ch**
39. **B–Kt3**	**P–R4**
40. **K×P**	**P–R5**
41. **B–Q6**	

And now the Bishop is on a "focus" square, where
it is loaded with the task of guarding both White's
Pawns, so cannot move without loss.

| 41. . . . | **K–K3** |
| 42. **K–B1** | **B–Q4!** |

At last! White must lose a second Pawn and the
game. Play went 43. **B–Kt8, R×P(QR6)**; 44. **R–K1ch,
K–B2**; 45. **R–B1ch, R–B6**; 46. **R×R, B×R**; 47.
K–Q2, P–KKt4; 48. **K–K3, B–B3**; 49. **B–B7,
K–Kt3**; 50. **B–Kt6, K–R4**; 51. **K–B2, K–Kt5**; 52.
B–Q8, P–Kt4; 53. **B–K7, B–Kt2**; 54. **K–K3, B–B1**;
55. **K–K4, K–R4**; 56. **K–K3, P–KKt5**; 57. **K–B2,
P–Kt6ch**; 58. **P×P, P–R6**; 59. **B–Q6, K–Kt5**;
60. **B–Kt4, B–Kt2**; 61. **K–Kt1, K×P**; and White
resigned.

Fourth Illustration

In the same tournament Euwe reached the following position against Milner–Barry after 45 moves—

46. **P–R5**

A malicious trap.

46. . . .   **B × P?**

47. **K–B2**

Threatening both P–Kt3ch and R–B6ch–B5ch.

47. . . .   **K–K4**

With or without check, 48. P–Kt3 wins the game. If 47 . . . B–Kt3ch, then 48. R × B, P × R; 49. P–Kt3ch. There followed 48. **P–Kt3, R × P;** 49. **K–Kt2, R–R4;** 50. **R–R6, B–Kt3;** 51. **B–Kt6,** and Black resigned.

Fifth Illustration

DR. M. EUWE   S. FLOHR
White   *Black*

(From the A.V.R.O. tourney.)

24. **P–B5 !!**

Threatening Kt–B4 and also P–B6 in some eventualities.

24.	. . .	P×P
25.	**Kt–B4**	**Q–Q1**

Neither 25 . . . Kt×KtP (26. Kt–Kt6, R×R; 27. R×R, Q–Q1; 28. Kt×R, Q×Kt; 29. P–Q6 followed by R–Q1 and possibly B–R3) nor 25 . . . Q–B2 (26. P–Q6, followed by Kt×P and B×P) would be any improvement.

26.	**Kt×P**	**Kt×KtP**
27.	**P–Q6**	**R×R**

If 27 . . . Q–B1, then 28. QR–Q1, threatening 29. B×P or 29. Kt–Kt6–K7ch or 29. P–Q7.

28. Q×Pch   K–R2

The alternative was 28 . . . K–R1; 29. R×R,
Q×P; 30. Kt–Kt6ch, K–R2; 31. Kt–K7, R–Q1 (if
31 . . . *R–B2*, then 32. *Q–Kt6ch* and *R–R8ch*); 32.
B–R3 with the deadly threat 33. B–B5ch. 32 . . . Q–Q5
would allow a thrilling finish. 33. B–B5ch, K–R1; 34.
R–K1, Q–Q7; 35. Kt–Kt6ch, K–R2; 36. Q×KKtPch!,
K×Q; 37. R–K7ch, K–Kt1; 38. B–K6 mate.

29. R×R   Q×P

The threat was 30. B×P, R–QKt1; 31. B–B3
followed by R–R7. And 29 . . . Q–K1 would succumb
to 30 . . . P–Q7. White's next move makes a crash.

30. B–K4ch!   K–R1

Or 30 . . . Kt×B, 31. Q–B5ch, etc.

31. Kt–Kt6ch   K–R2
32. Kt–K7ch   Black resigned

A combination in Euwe's very best style. The initial
sacrifice was perfectly sound, and the whole combination went through with murderous exactitude.